PARIS UNDERGROUND

The dark side of the city of light

Photography by Alain Bali

ISBN 10 : 1939204623
ISBN 13 : 978-1-939204-62-2

ACKNOWLEDGEMENT

I would like to thank the Paris City Hall, for providing me the necessary authorizations and clearances to conduct this work.
Also I want to thank Marc, Christian, Tintin, and Eric for taking me places I was not allowed to go.

CONTENT:

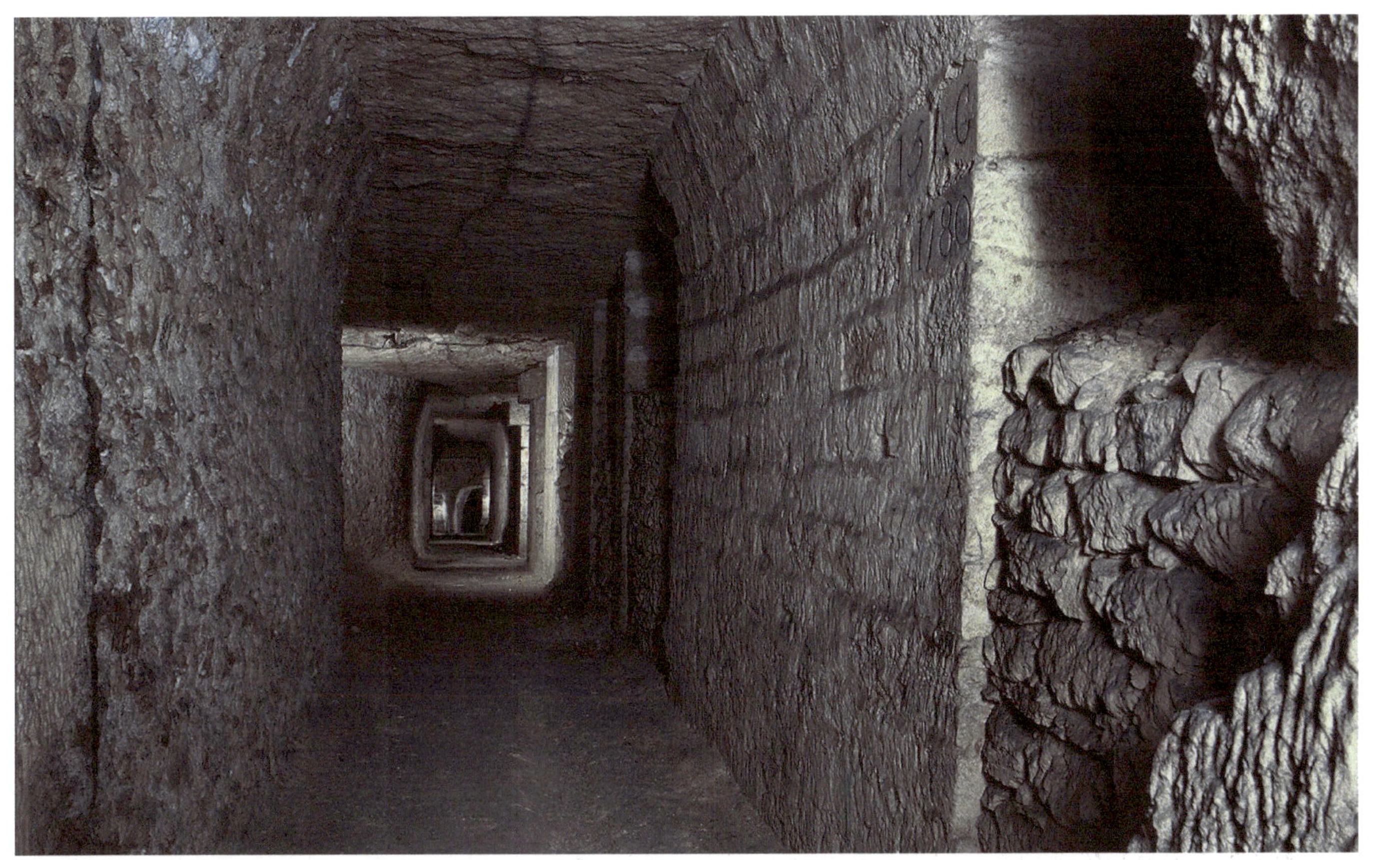

PARIS UNDERGROUND was the first photographic extensive reportage of the underground network under Paris: (catacombs, quarries, metro subway system, sewers, shelters, canals), and many bizarre places. Hundreds of kilometers underground galleries have been waiting hundreds of years to be discovered.

The access to the quarries has always been forbidden and still is today. Only a few secret entrances are known by a few "cataphiles" usually a simple manhole in a street that nobody would have suspected to be the entrance to an unchartered world below ...

As a result of this literary masterwork, these subterranean spaces have become a major focus for urban culture and creativity, resulting in a private, inspirational source for visual arts, music and writing.

Alain Bali

Image: Service gallery under the cross of Alesia and Tombe Issoire Street

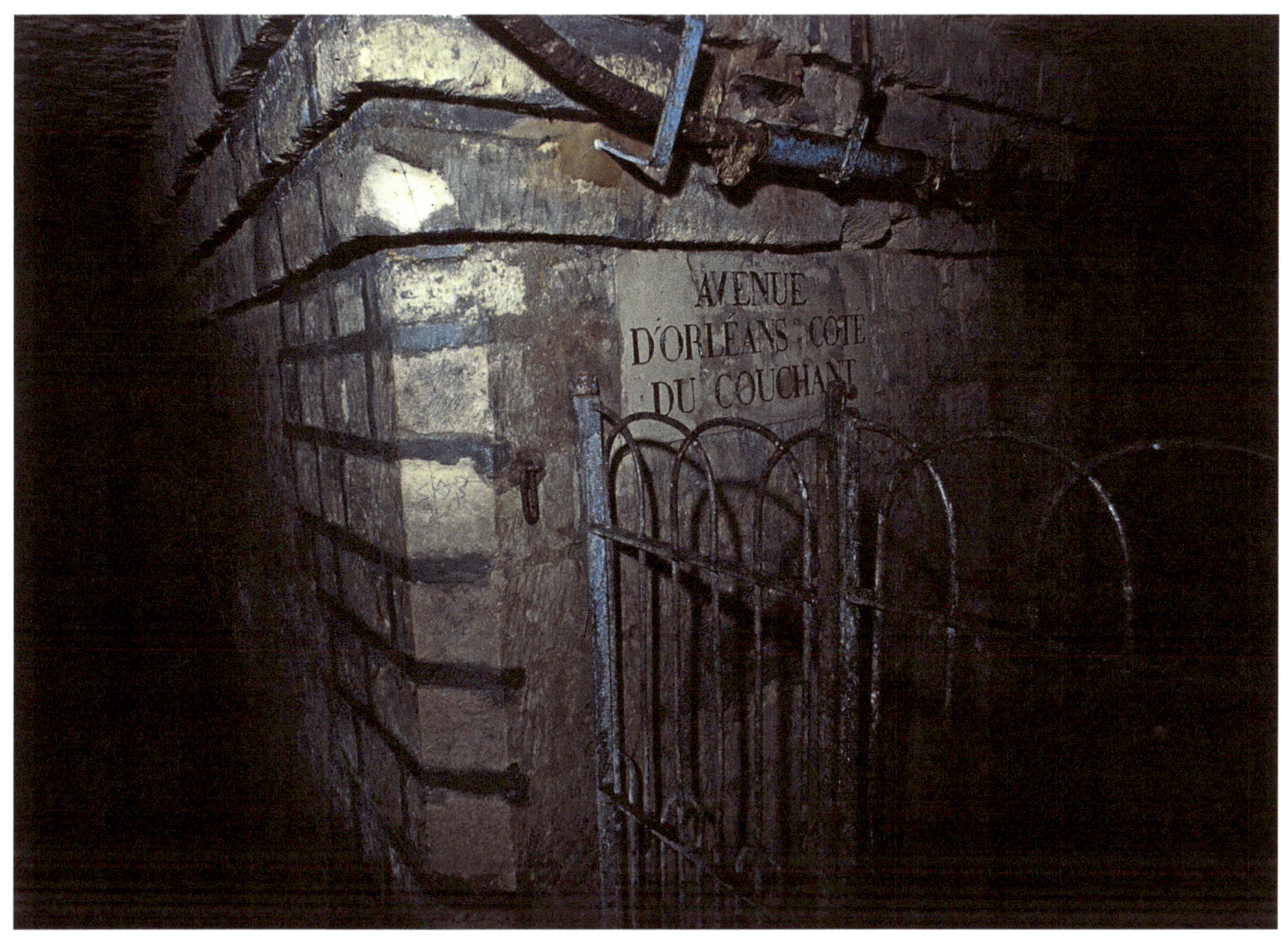

CHAPTER ONE : THE QUARRIES

Out of 220 miles of obscure galleries have been extracted hundred tons of stones to build the City of Light. After the book publication and the following media coverage, it became a trendy for Parisians to experience the thrill of a lawless underground territory. People organized parties, concerts, art events, spiritual gatherings, devil-worshipping ceremonies etc.

It started with the collapse of a building, caving in at street level. The dramatic event triggered the decision to create the “IGC, Inspection Generale des Carrieres”, (Inspectorate General of Underground Quarries), in 1777, which duty was to map the quarries and consolidate weak spots. Everyone came to realize that Paris was sitting on Gruyere cheese subsoil, and without a map no one would dare to wander in a dark multi level labyrinths.

In order to contain the phenomenon, the City of Paris had to create a special Police unit to prevent access to the quarries by patrolling on the weekends.

I was myself once chased and arrested a gunpoint under the Hospital Blvd, in the 13 the district. The reason (I was told at the police station), was that I was in a gallery right under the main Police Database Center building, fact of course I did not know …

Another time I got lost under the Chaillot hill.
A small hill facing the Eiffel Tower with on the right side of the Seine River, with on top a famous theater. I was searching for whatever was left of a Chinese temple, built in the quarries for the celebration of the Universal Exposition of 1900. After wandering for hours, I could not find the temple, or my way out. I realized that I was walking in circles and there was no indication on my map of a ladder or staircase that could get me back to street level.
As I was getting desperate, I heard some faint voices coming from the other side of the gallery wall. I decided to dig a hole in the wall with my crowbar to escape a sure death. The stone was soft and humid, I was progressing fast. So fast that all of a sudden the wall collapsed, and I fell into the other side, finding myself in middle of a group of 20 persons dressed in Roman gladiator costumes.
I had crashed into a rehearsal of a play in the Theater of Chaillot. Everyone was stunned and frozen staring at me as if I was some kind of devil popping out of a box, it gave me enough time to quickly dust off my jacket, readjust my glasses, gather my equipment and walked out through the theater main door.

The quarries have always been linked to extraordinary events.

At every epoch the quarries have been associated with devils, sorcerers. evil spirits and black magic. They have scared everyone away except smugglers, thieves , freedom fighters and revolutionaries, who always found in Paris's belly a perfect place to hide.

Some con artists were offering to gullible clients a "meeting with the Devil". Once in the darkness of a tunnel, an accomplice with fake horns stuck on his head would appear briefly in a candle light screaming and making faces. Cheap thrill guaranteed, worth every gold coin paid.

Philibert Aspairt was a doorman at the Val de Grace hospital. Out of curiosity on June 21 1791, he decided to explore the quarries down below the hospital. He took the beautiful stone carved staircase down to a 80 feet descent and he reached the first gallery and began his exploration.

Unfortunately, Philibert never found his way back. His remains were found 11 years later, he was identified by the sets of keys still attached to his belt.
In 1944 during the German occupation, the FFI (French freedom fighters) installed a secret headquarters under the Denfert Rochereau place in the 14th district, just under the German Kommandantur. From this underground location the liberation of France was launched.

Under the Saint-Anne Hospital the quarries were used to lock up psychiatric patients suffering of "dangerous dementia". The place was called " Cage a fou" (Cage for Crazy).

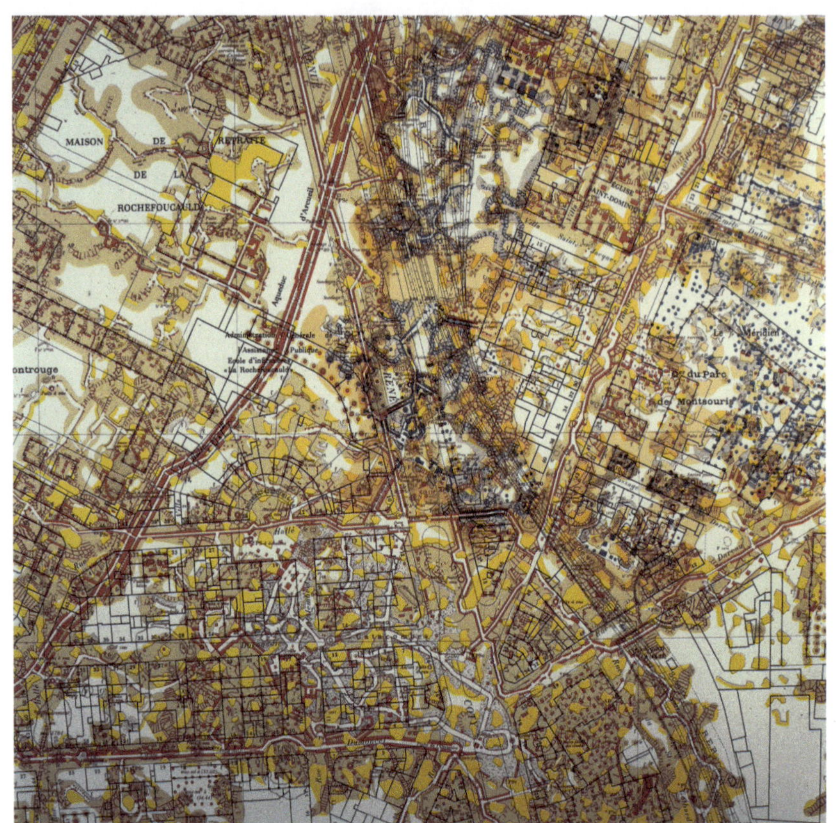

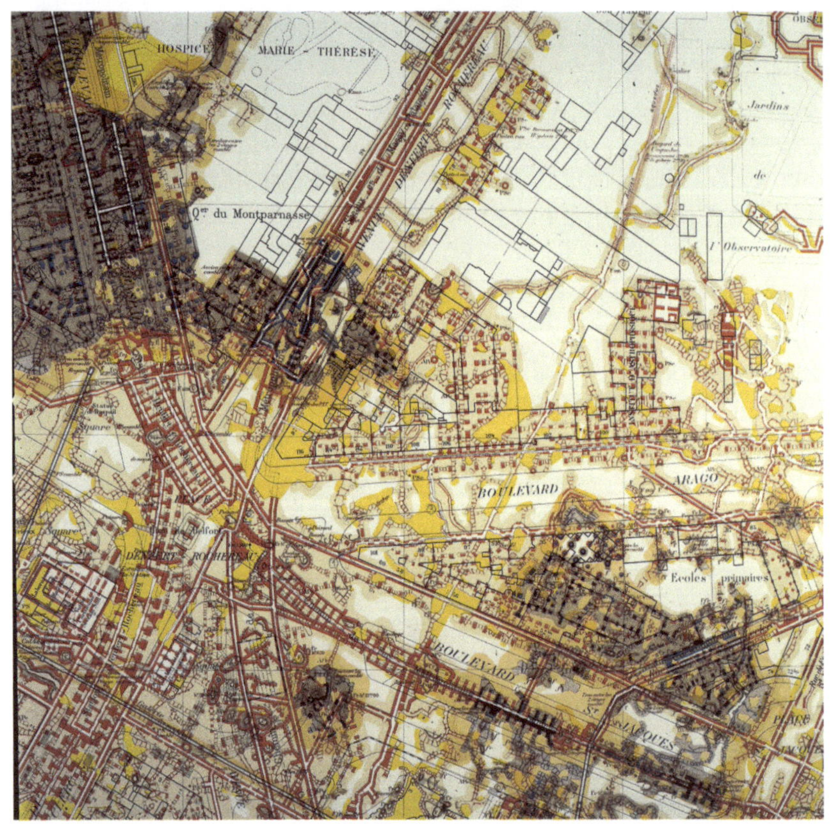

Map created by the Inspectorate General of Underground Quarries.

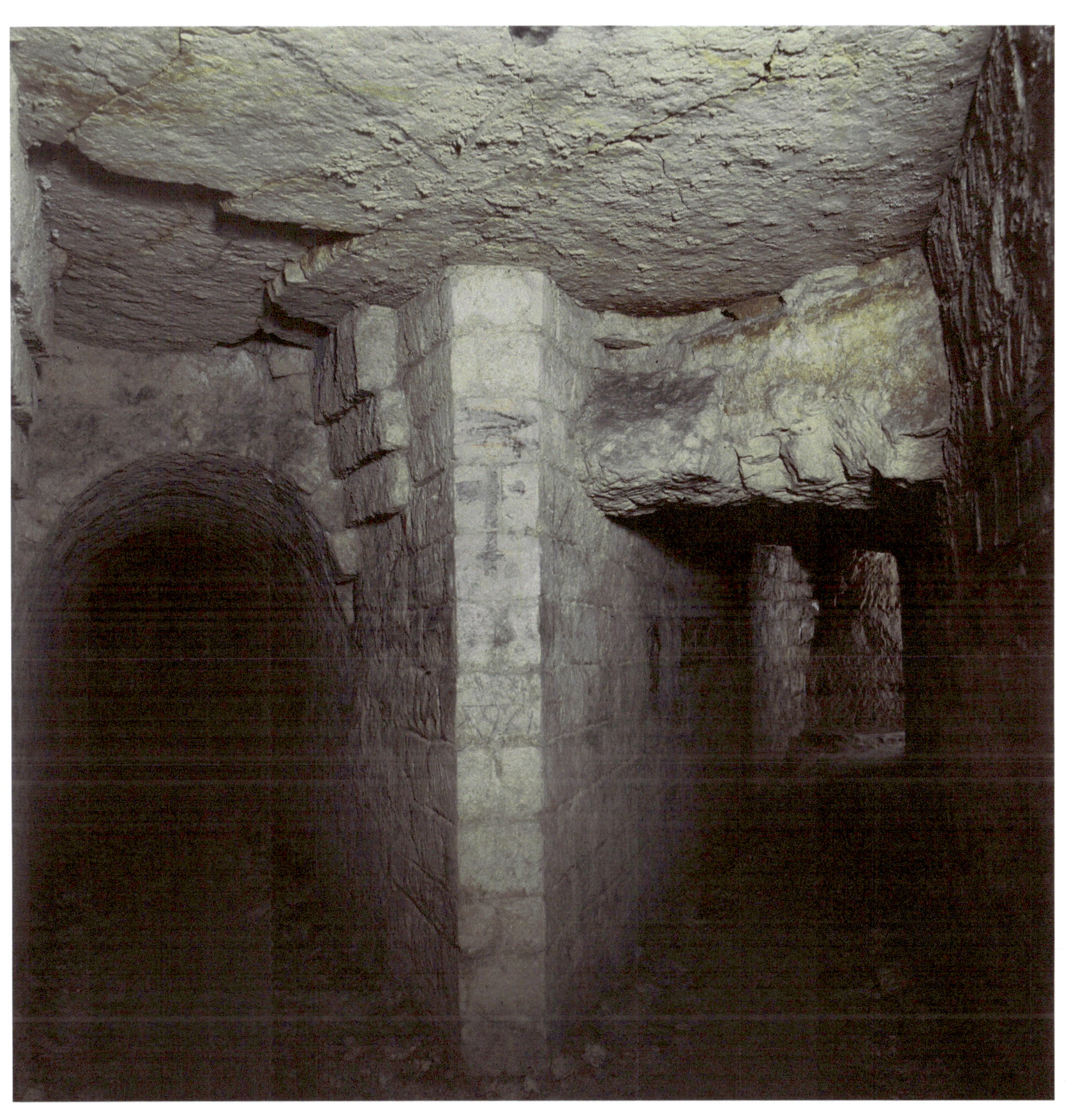

Example of the necessity to carry a map. Left or right ?

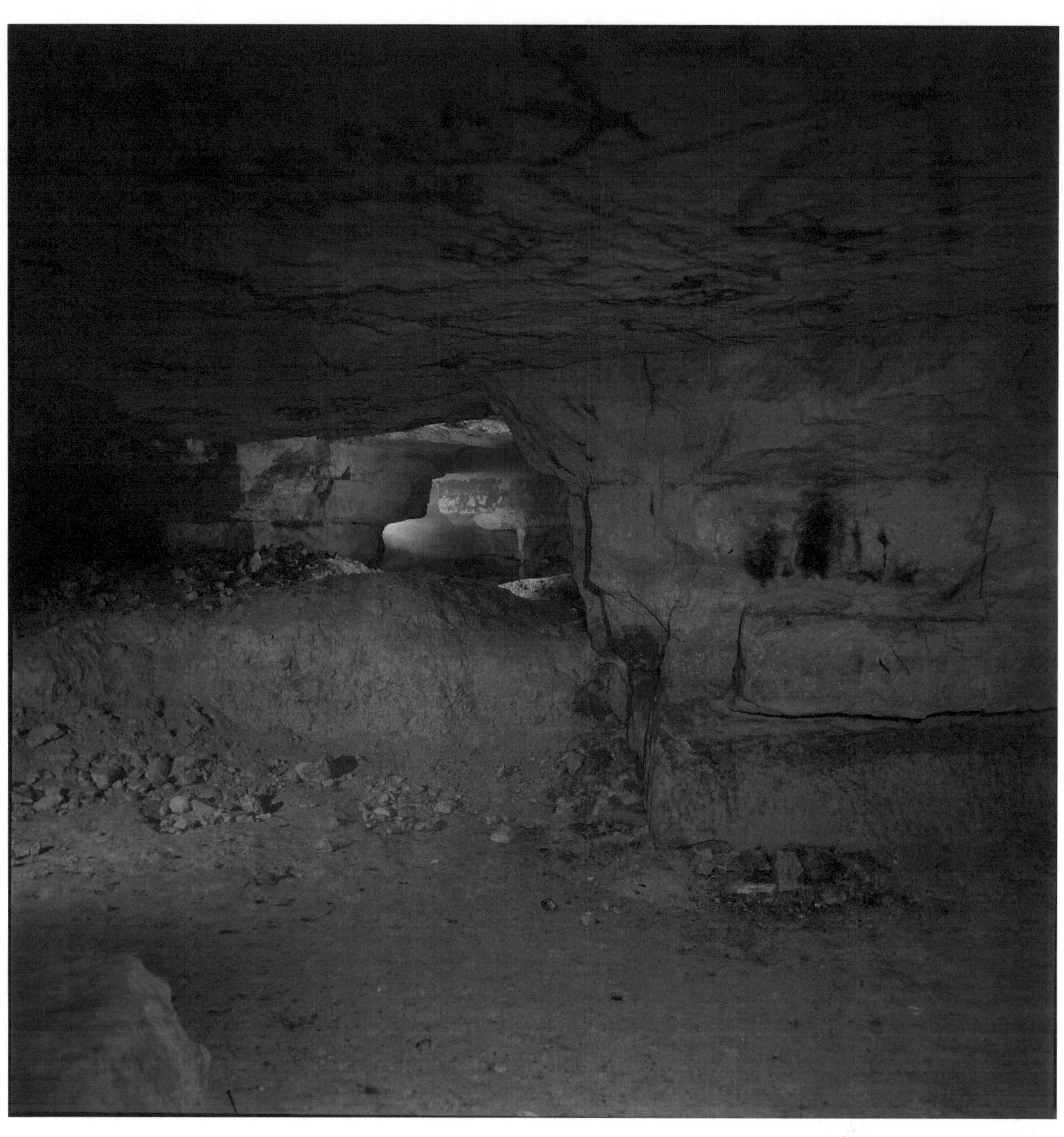

Port Mahon quarries, rounded pillars 10 feet high (3 meters).

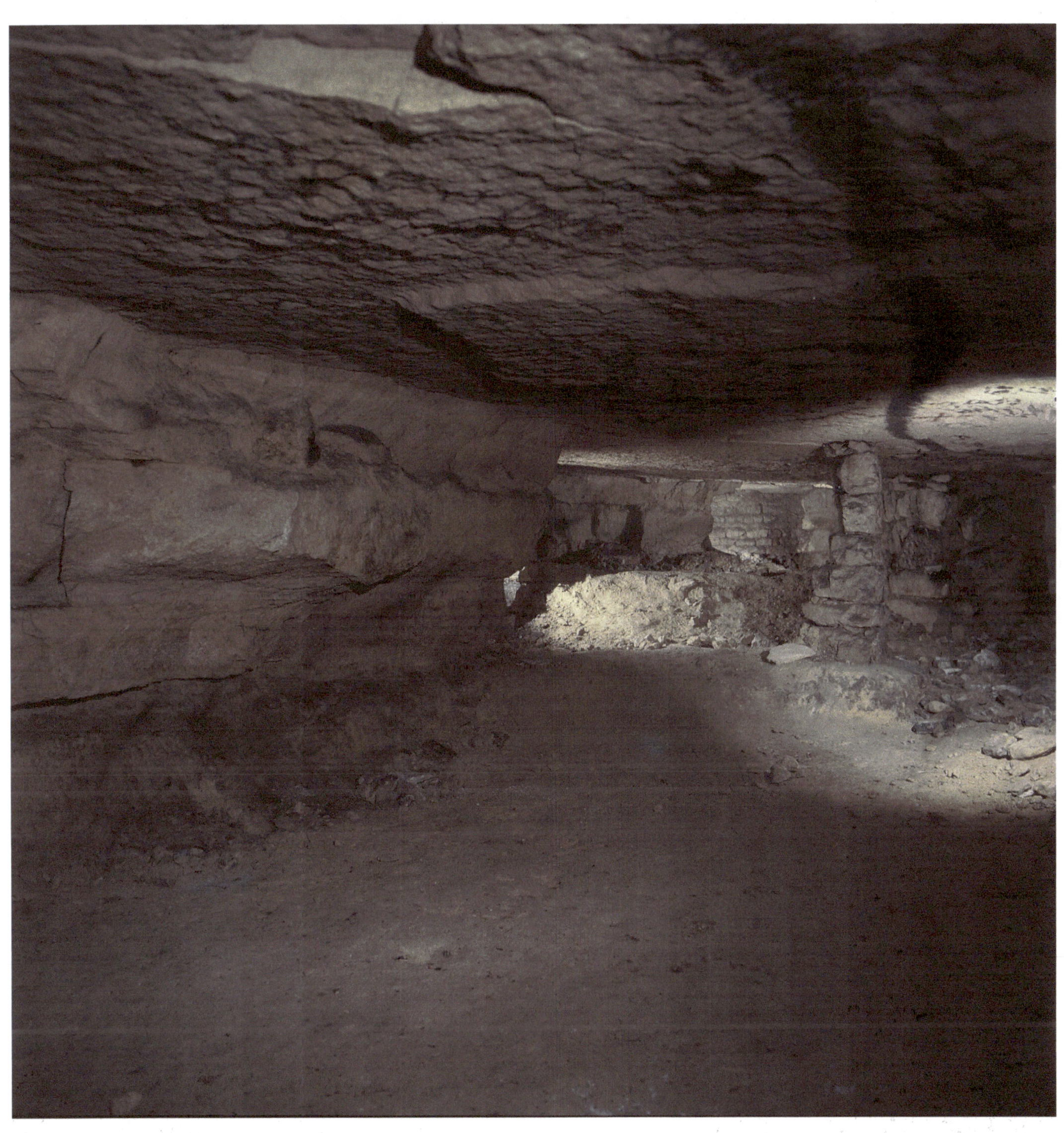

The underground quarry of Port Mahon is one of the oldest quarry under Paris. Its use dates back to the 15th century. It has been classified historical monuments on January 4, 1994..

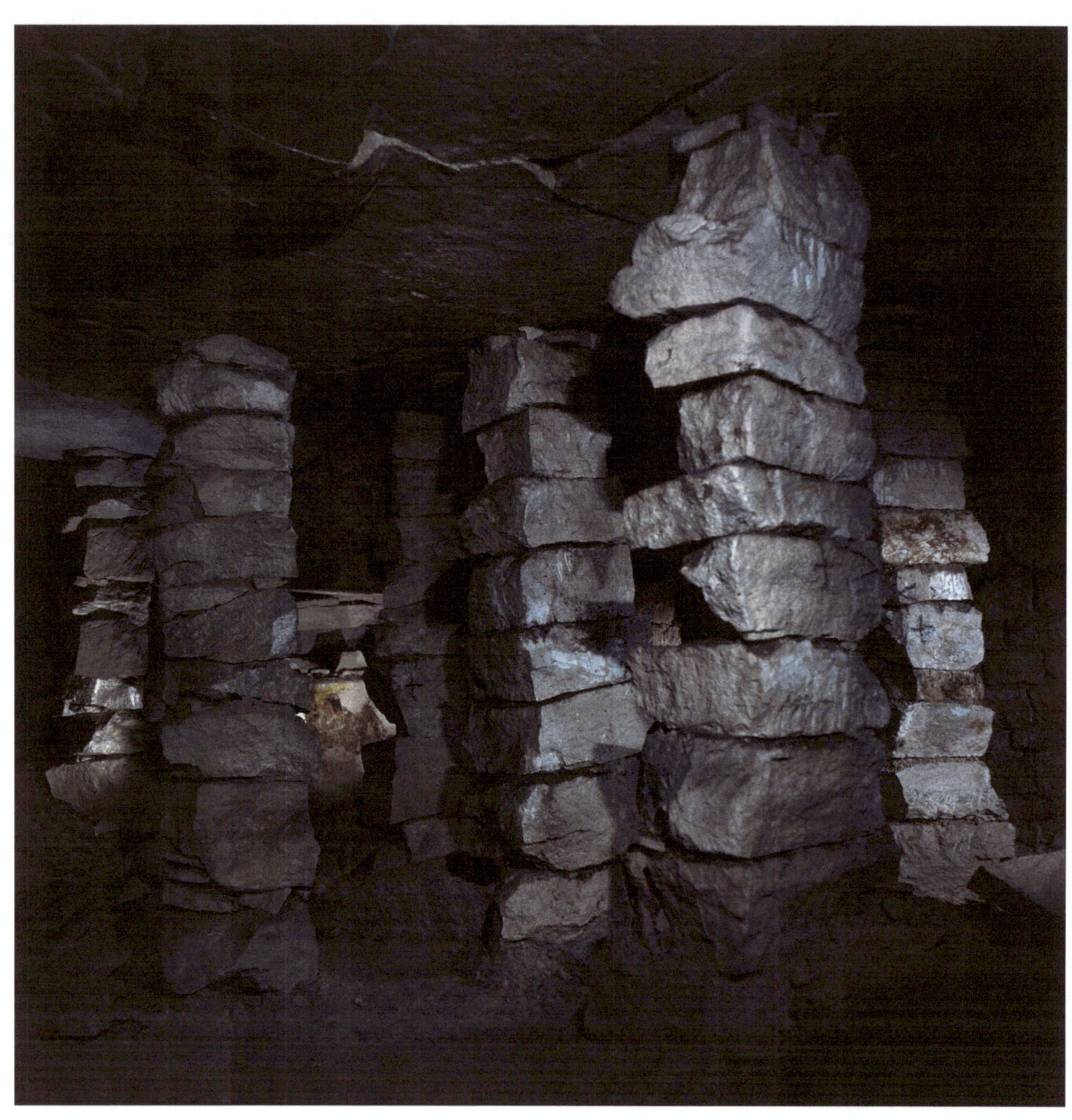

A forest of pillars in the lower level of the quarry of Port Mahon.

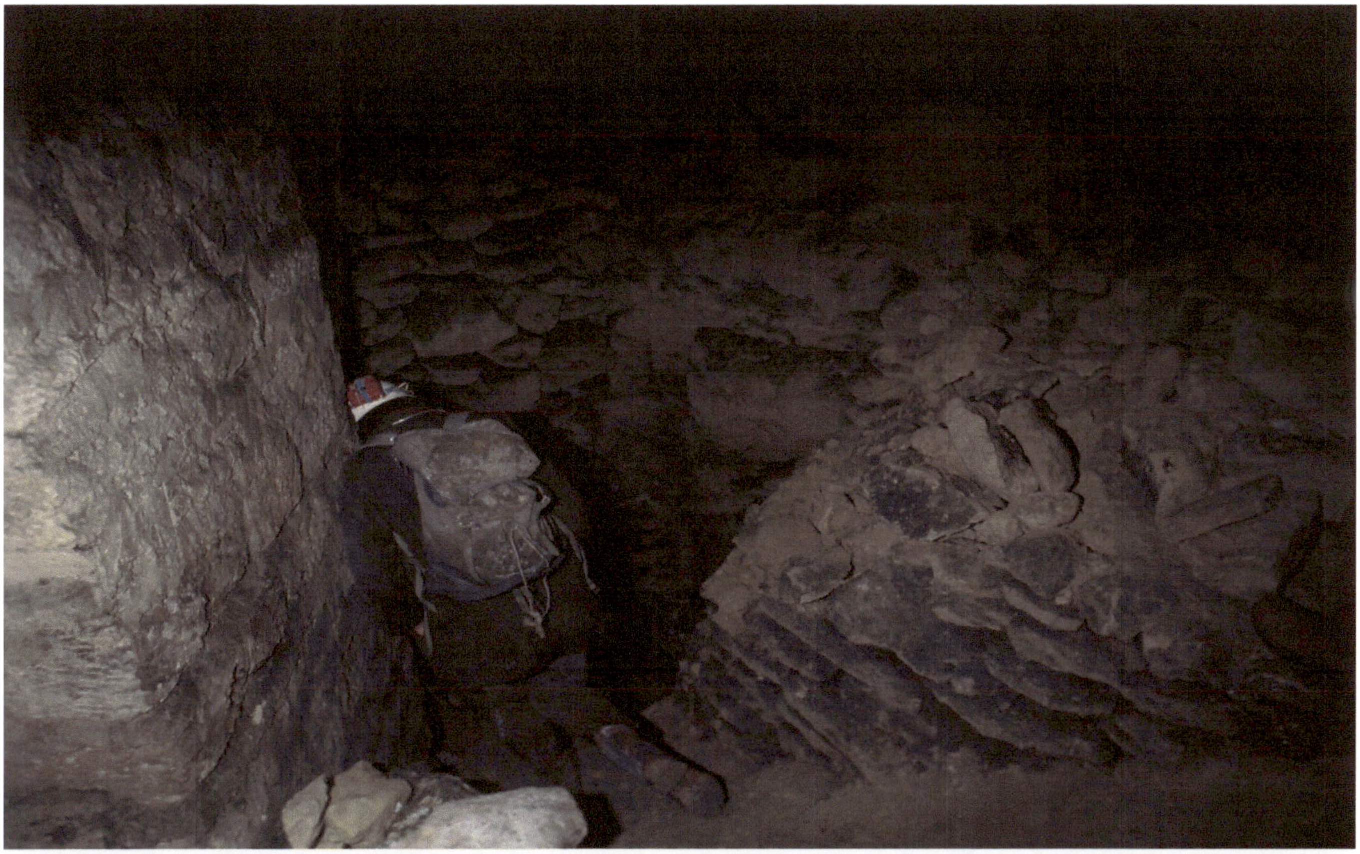

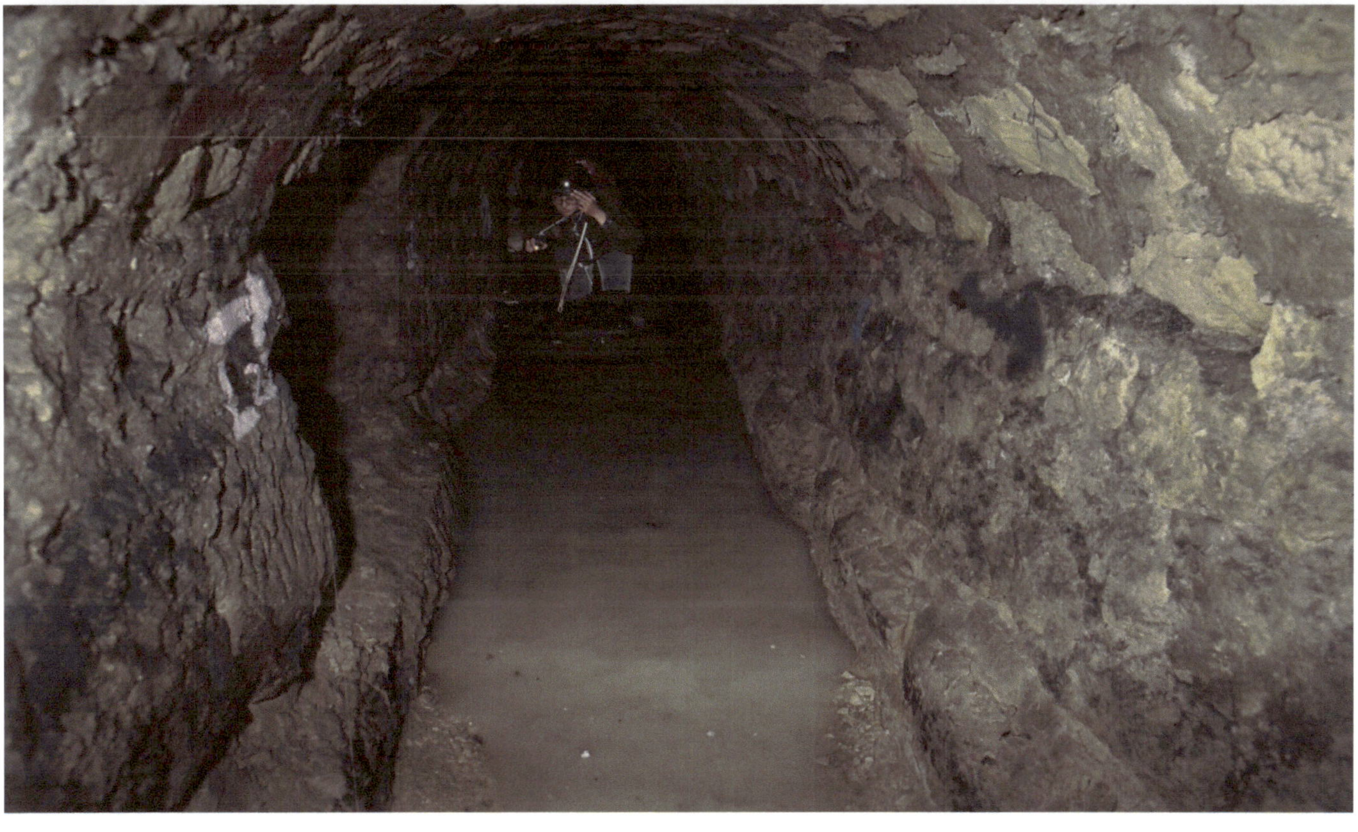

Descending to a lower level flooded gallery .

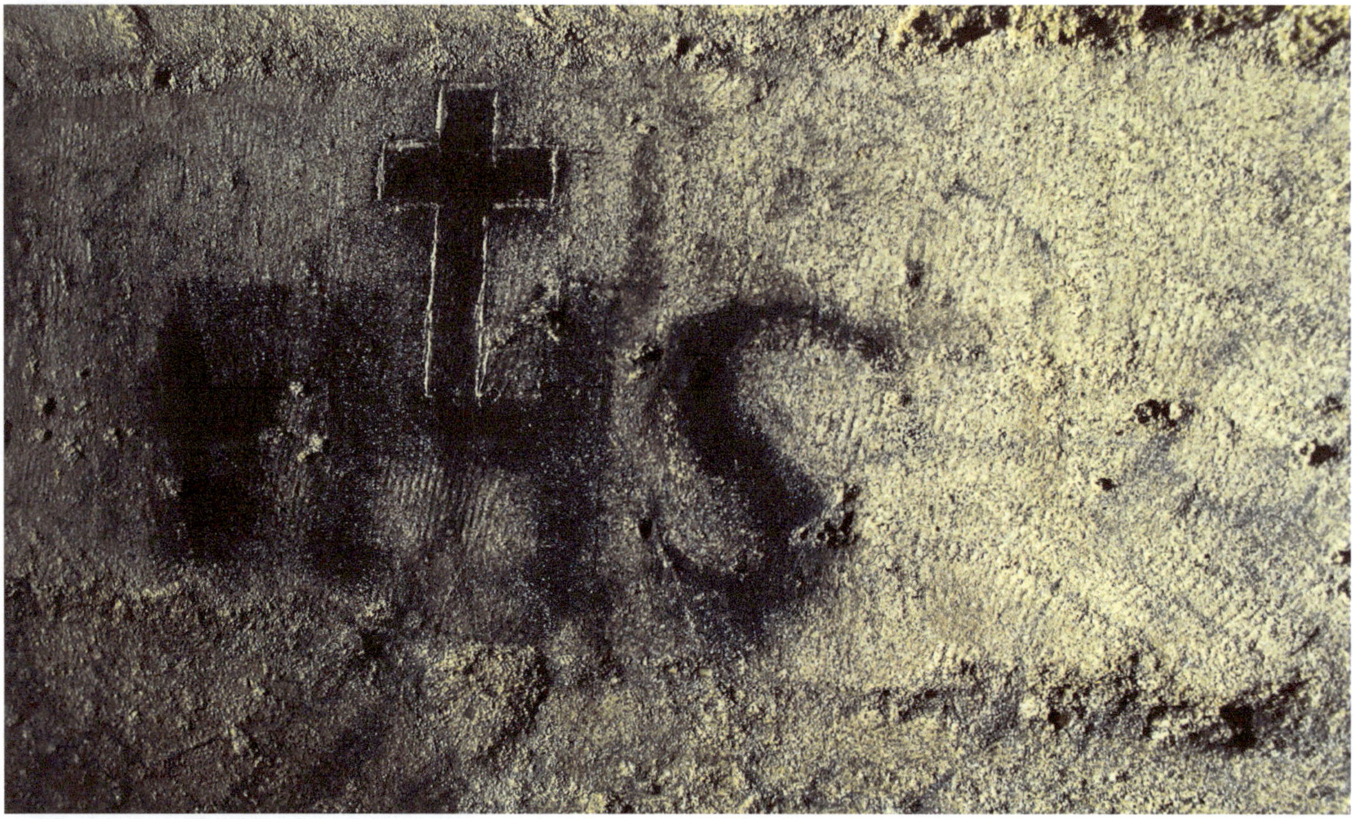

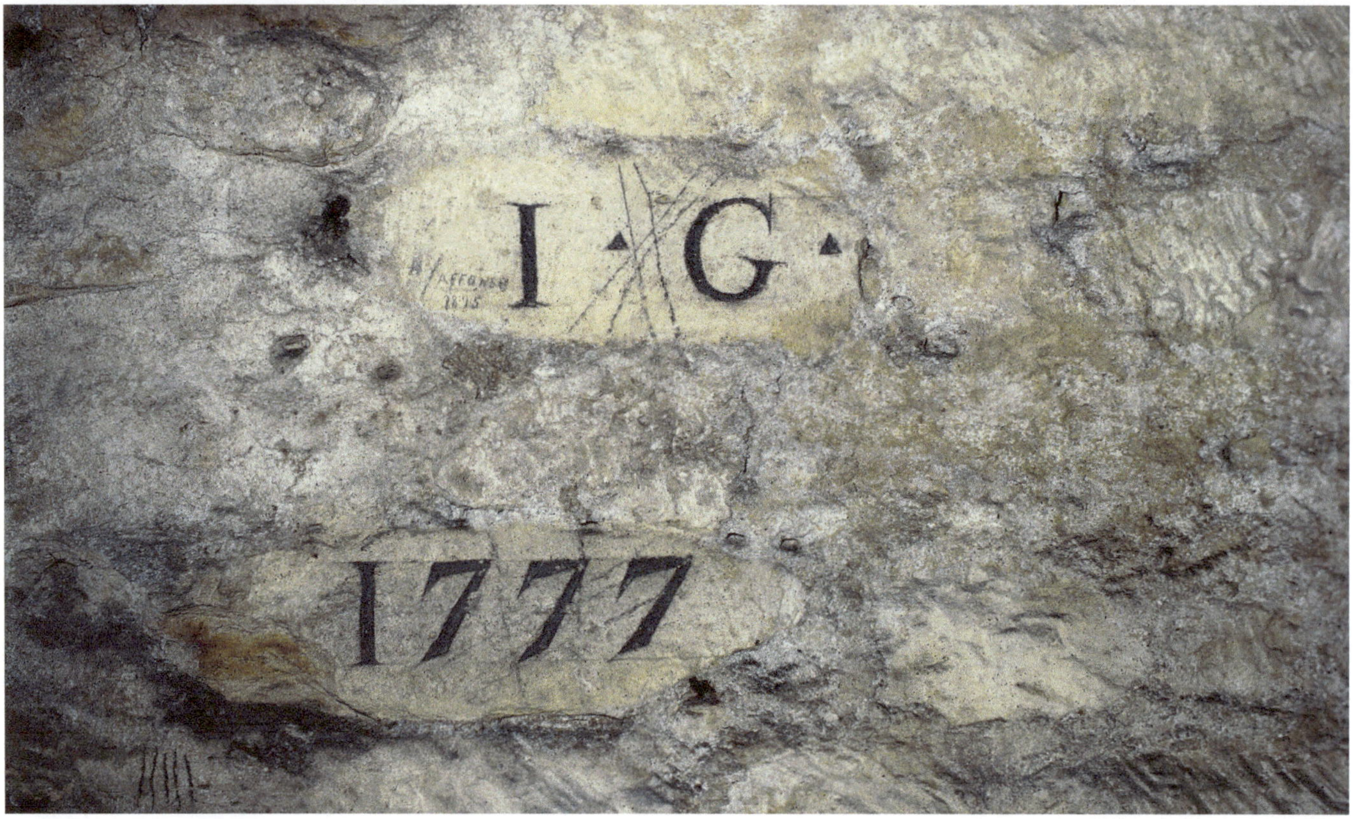

Carved sign making a fortification pillar: "I" for first stage, and "G" for Guillaumot who was the inspector in charge in 1777

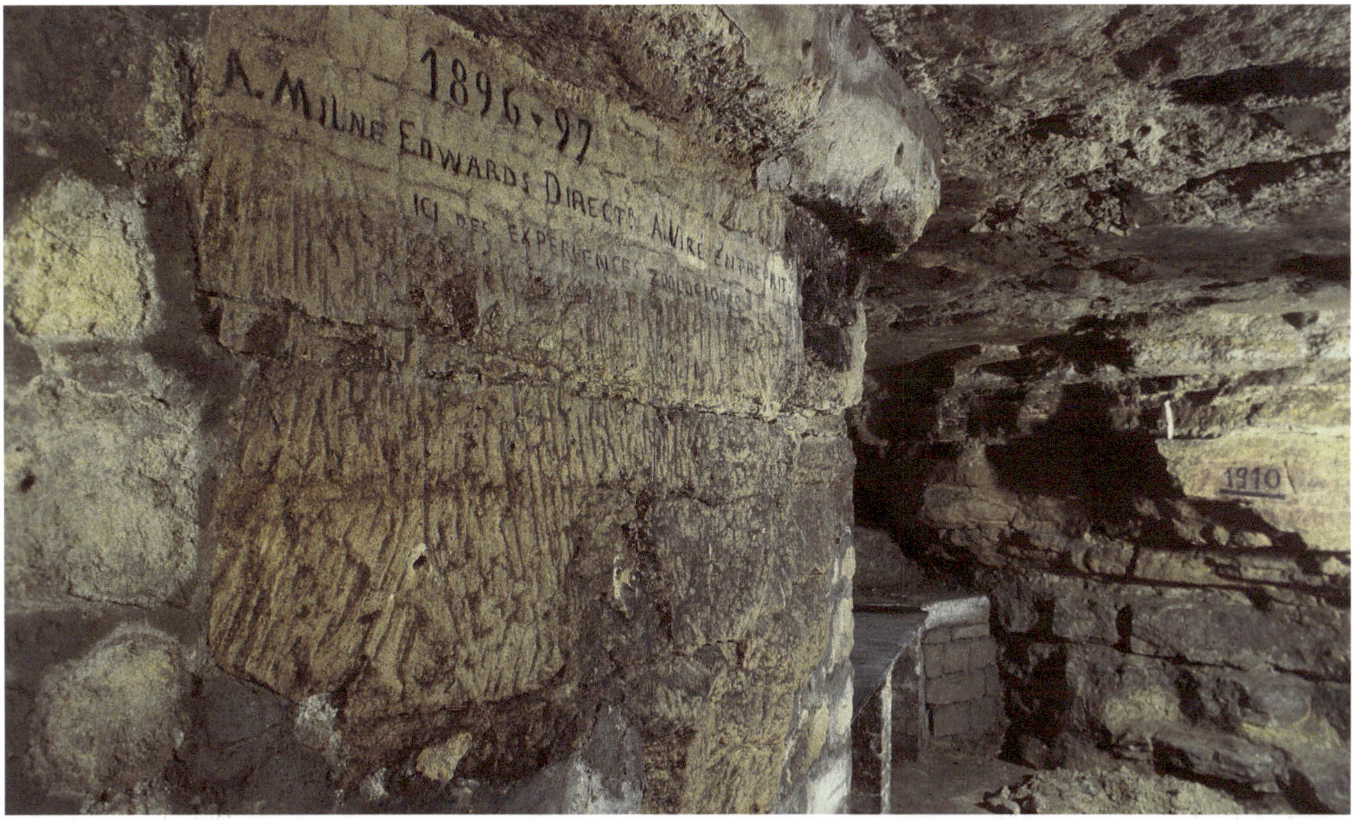

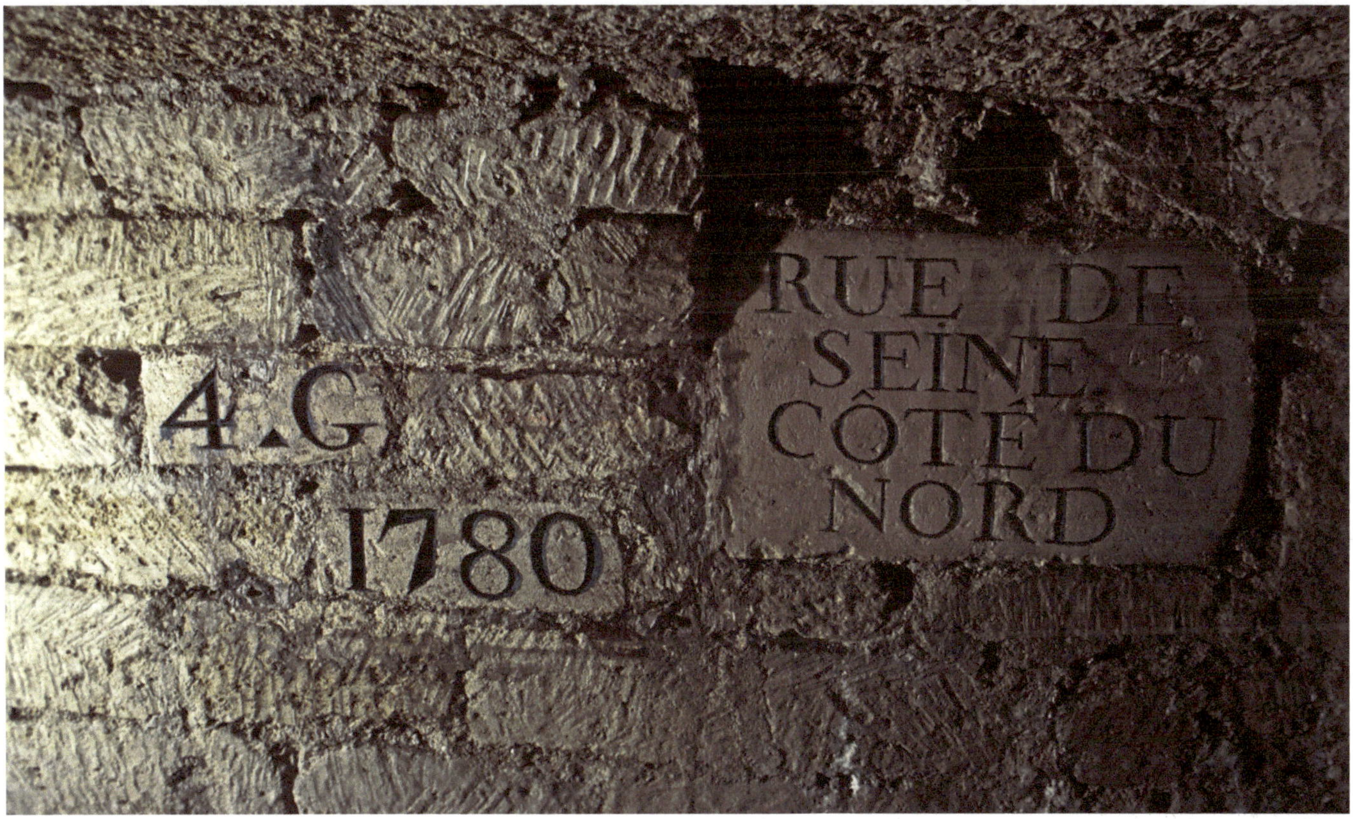

Indication of the above street name.

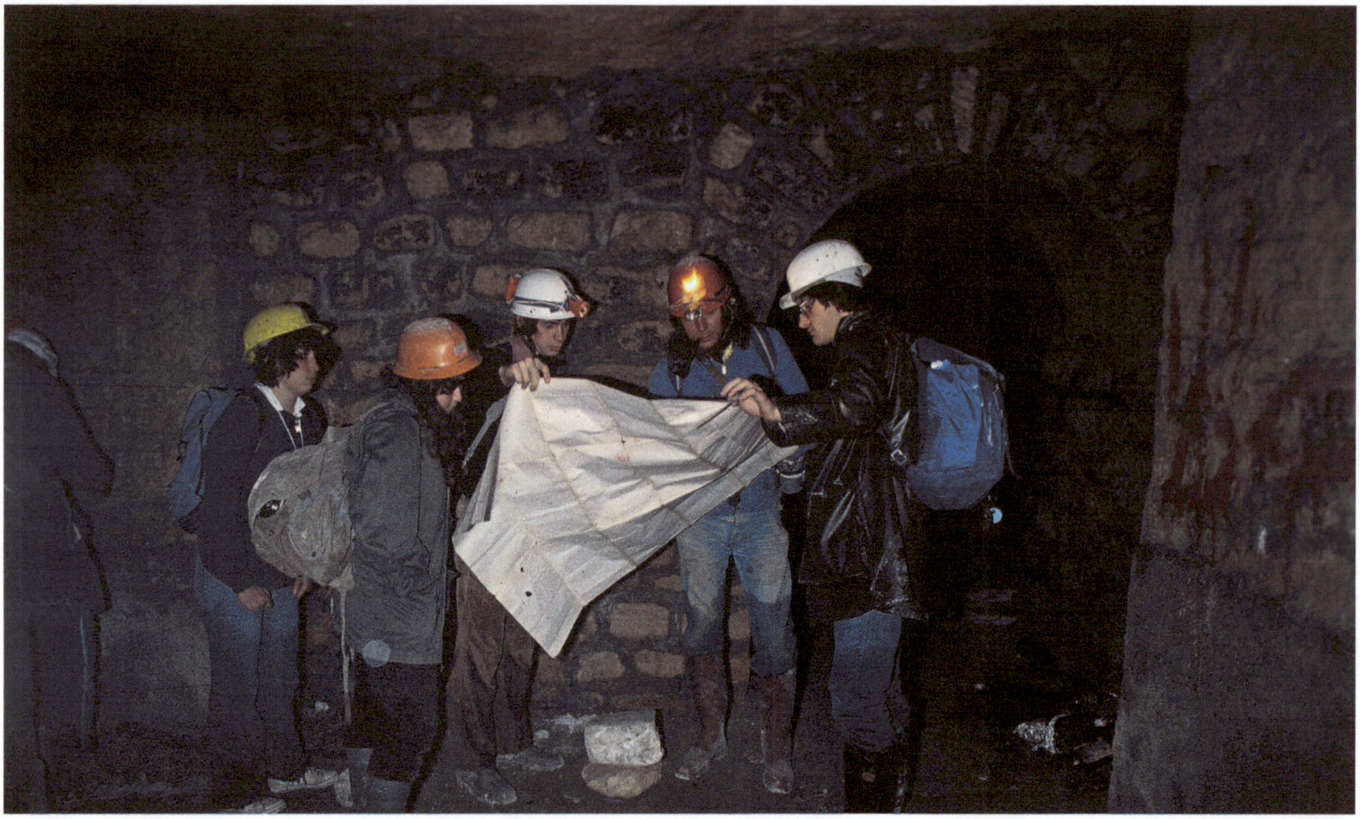

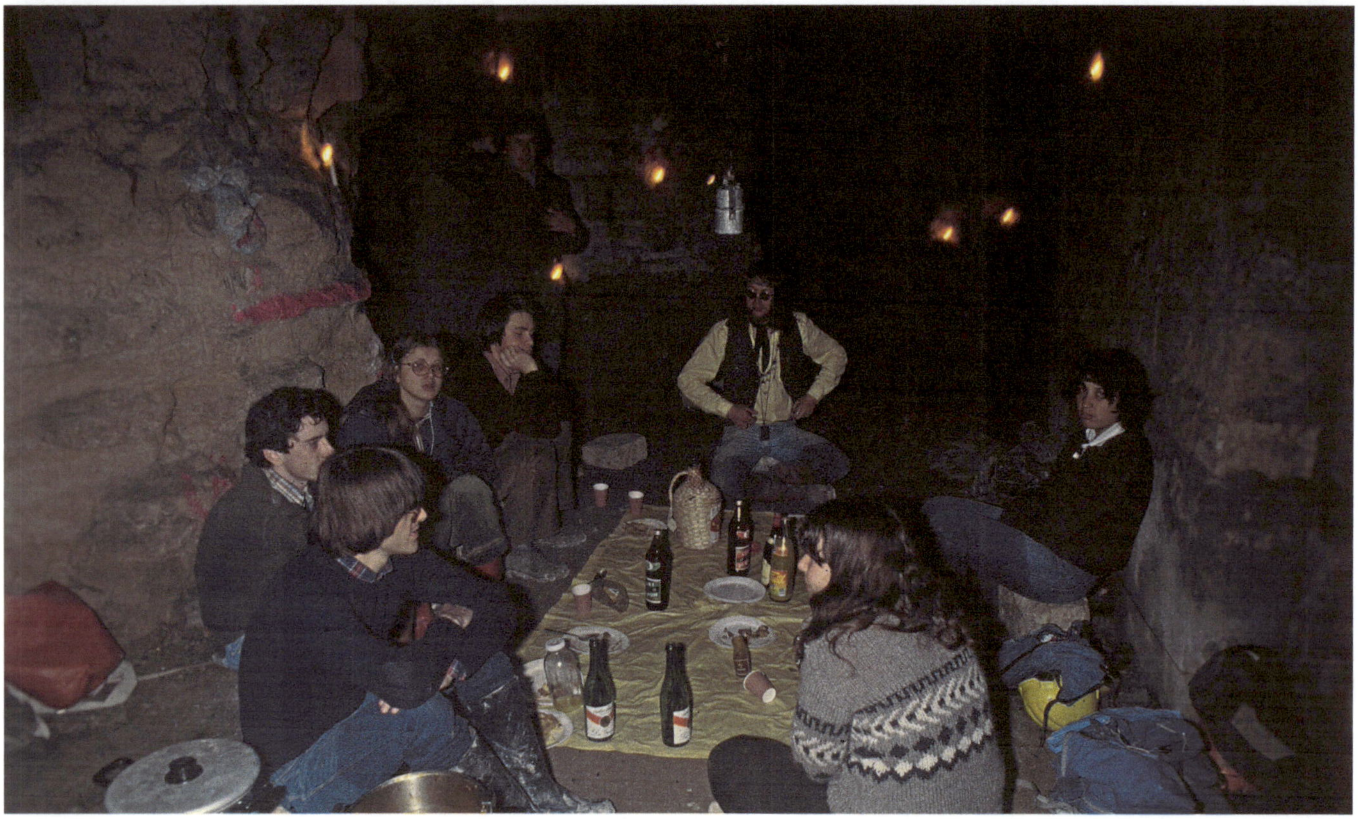

Orientation check up and picnic break

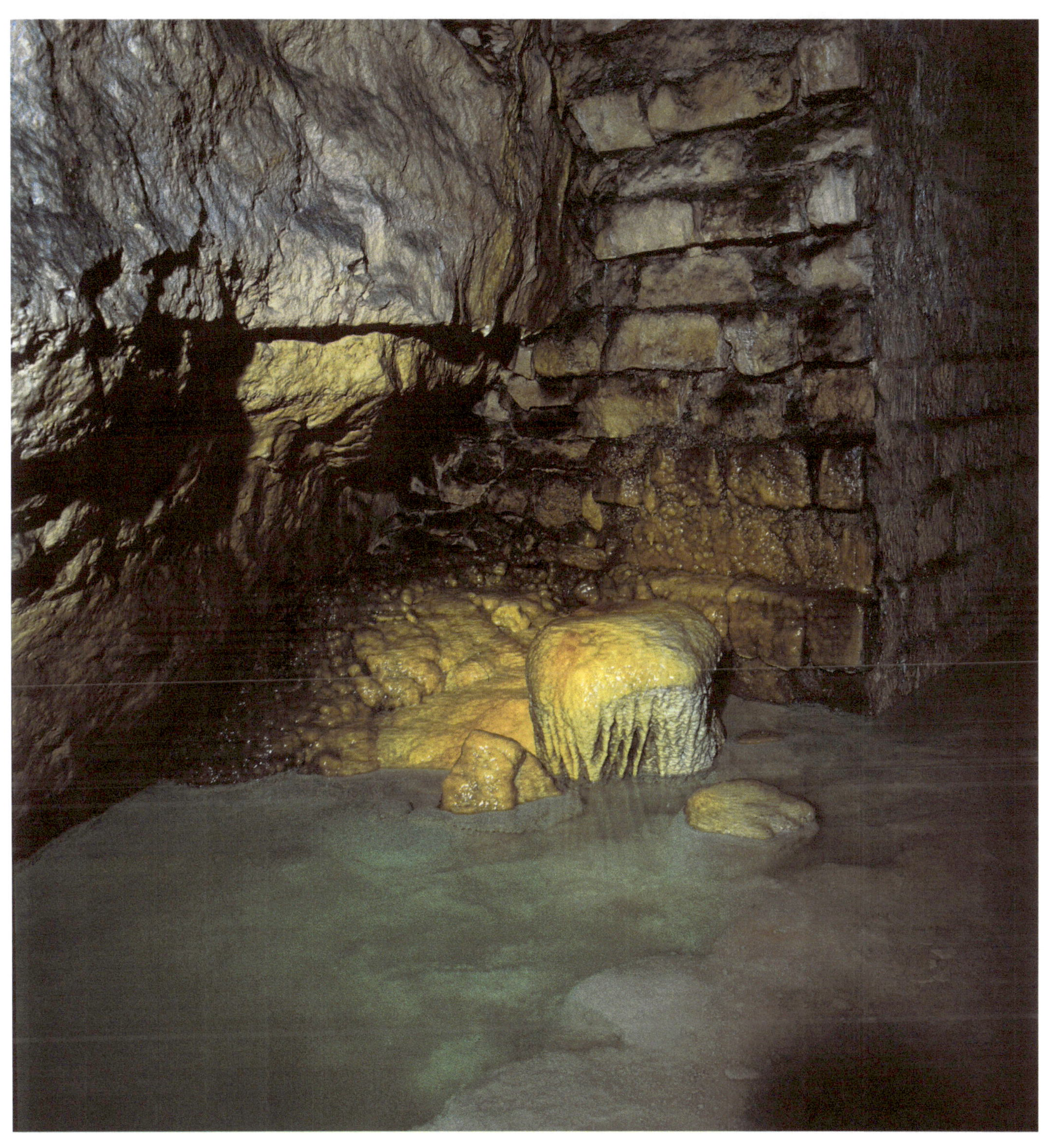

Reille Avenue, spring leak.

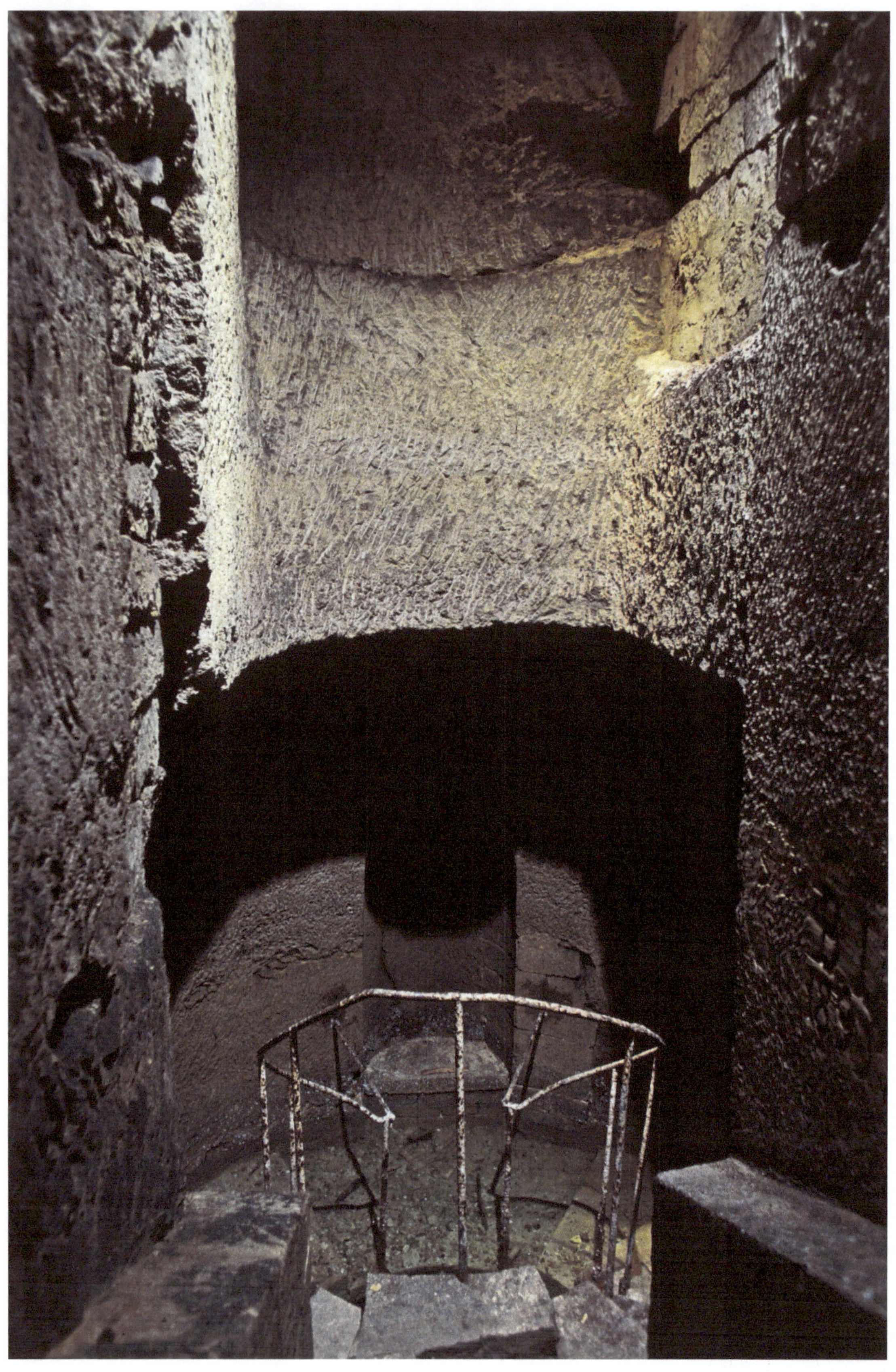

This place is called Quarrymen's footbath it is the first geological drilling in Paris, in the oldest medieval quarry of Port-Mahon, close to the official Paris catacombs.

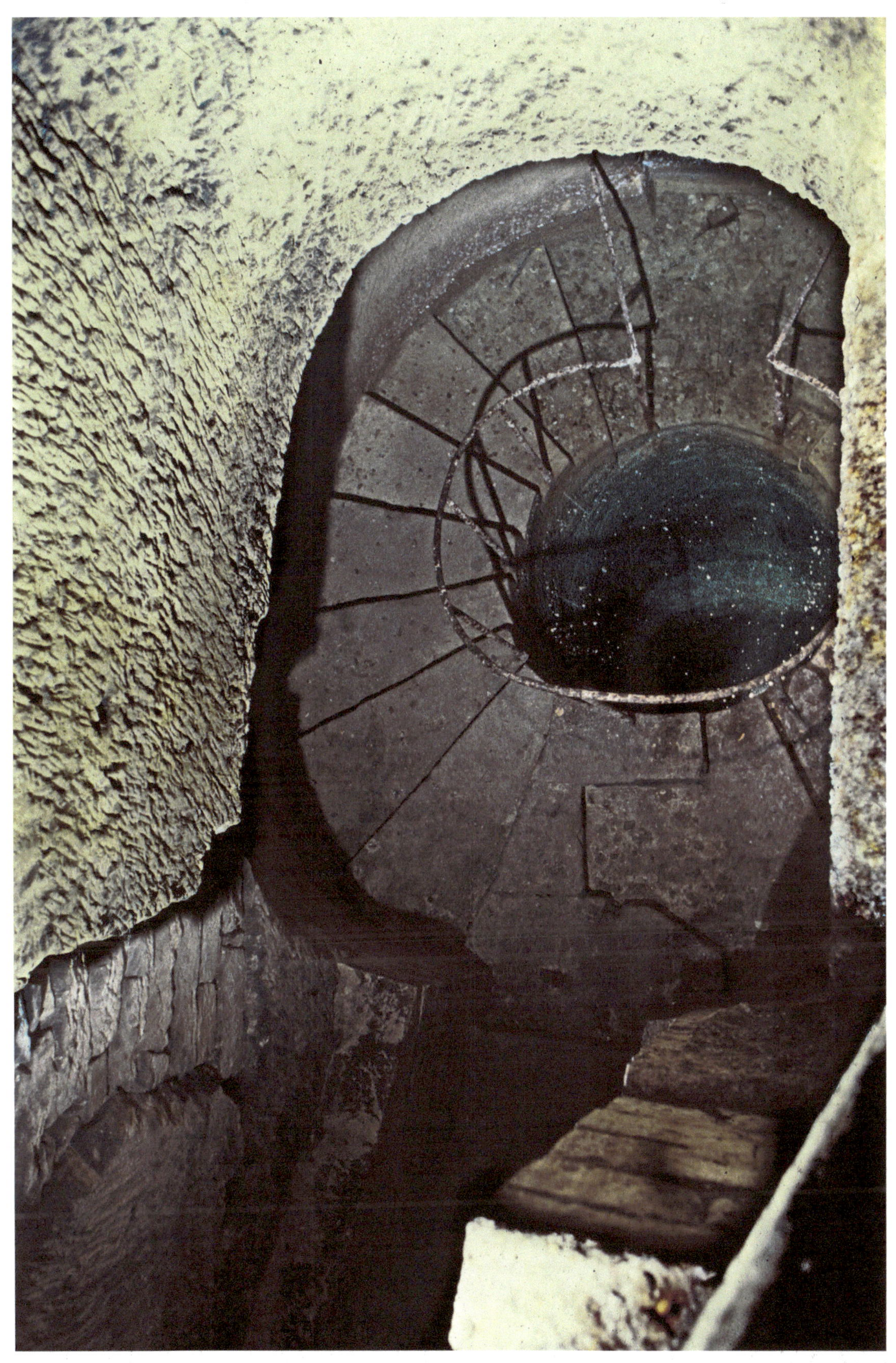

Quarrymen's footbath, above view.

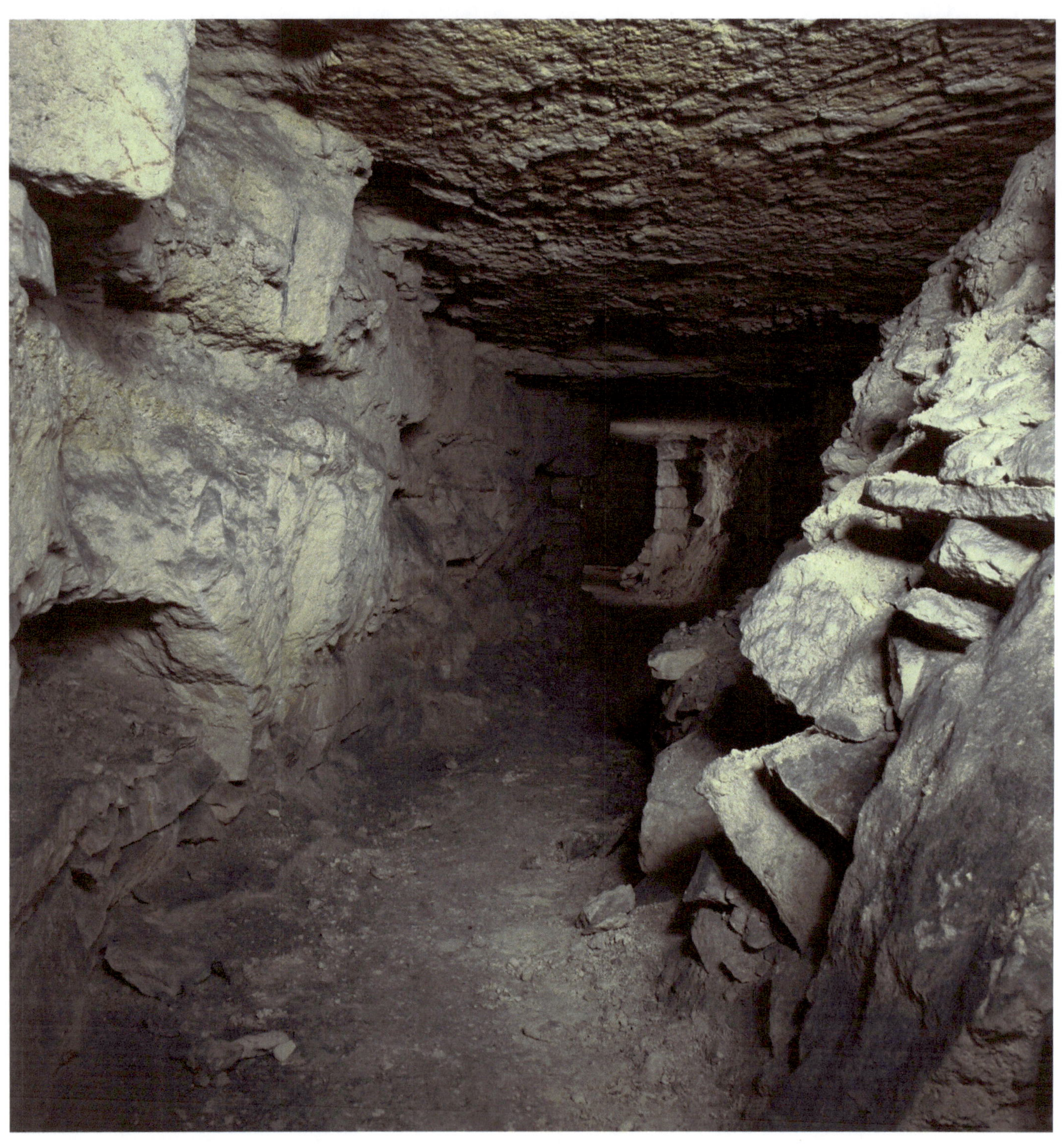

Gallery where stone extraction stopped.

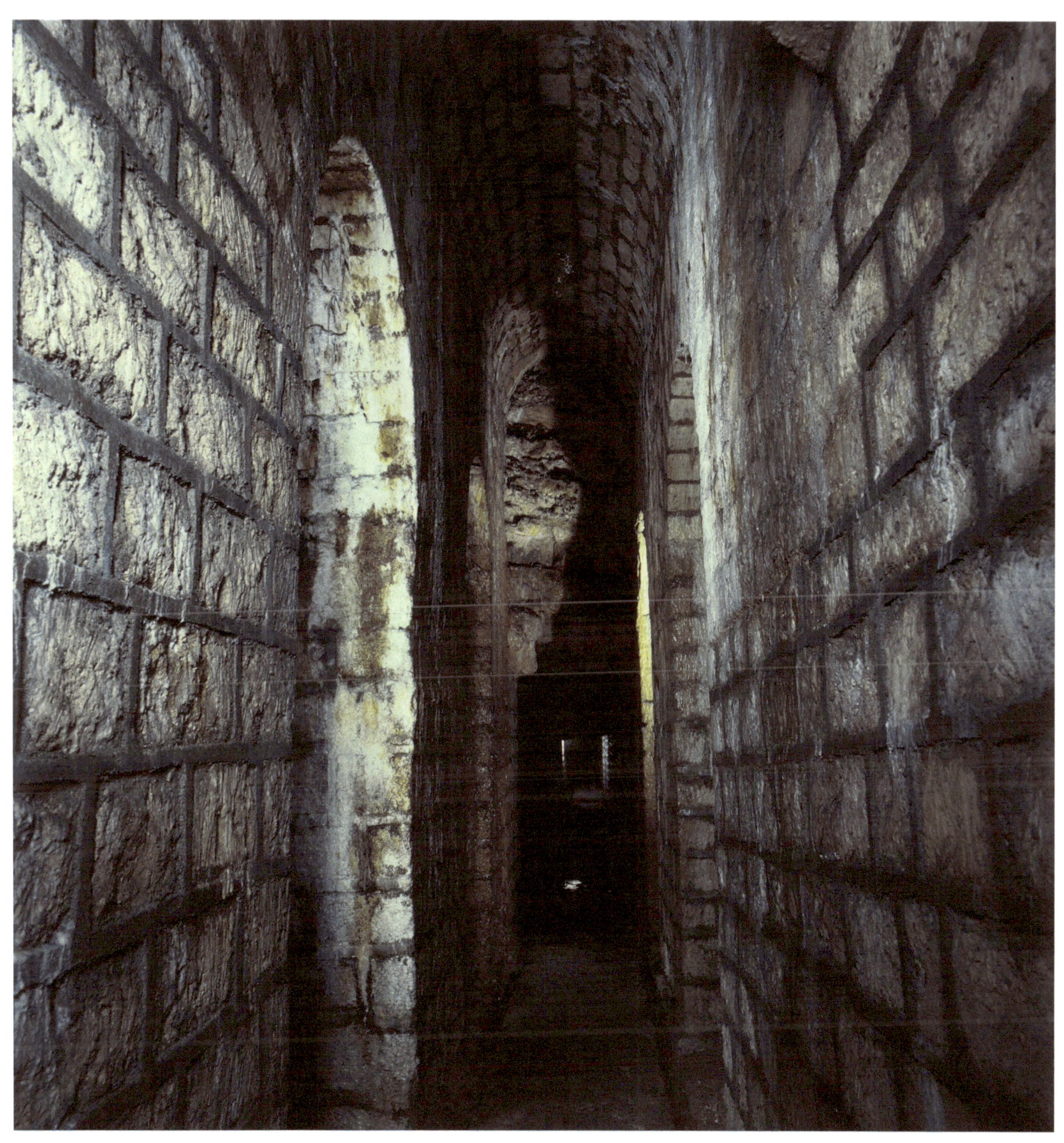

Consolidation under the Montsouris water reservoir.

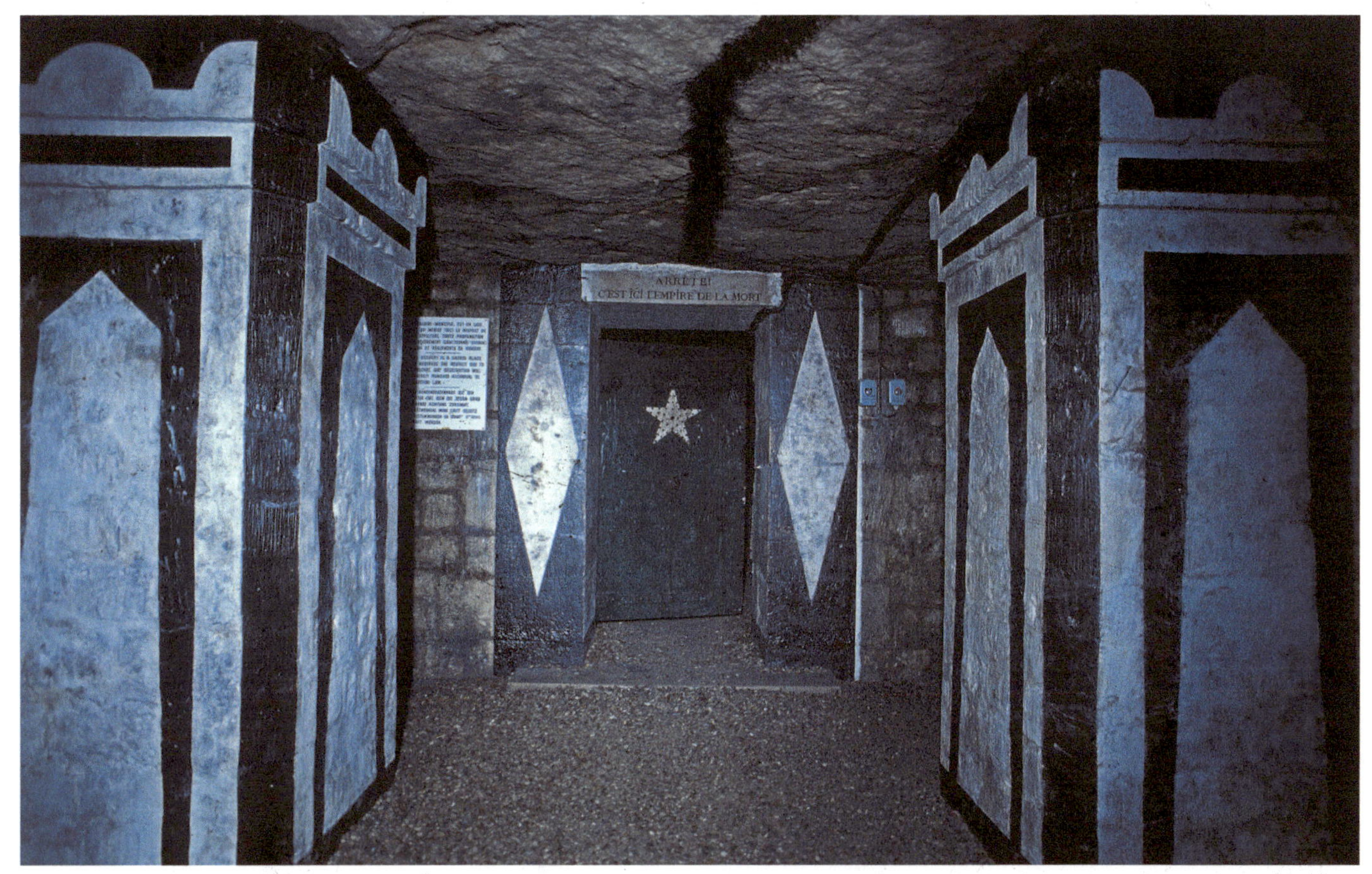

CHAPTER TWO: THE CATACOMBS

Paris 1785. All the cemeteries of the city were so overcrowded, that corps were popping out from their graves, even into the cellars of surrounding houses.
The deads were coming back to haunt the livings. Fearing the spread of deadly diseases, rats proliferation and other horrors, the decision was made to exhume the remains of some 6 millions Parisians and to dump them into the quarries.

Twelve years of bone filled wagons emptied the city's dead into the caverns below where they sat in piles and heaps for twenty-two more years until Louis-Étienne Héricart de Thury, decided to turn the bone piles into an artistic monument which also incorporated gravestones and funerary monuments un order to show remains'provenances.

Main Catacombs entrance. The sign above the door reads:"Stop here, it is the Empire of Death"

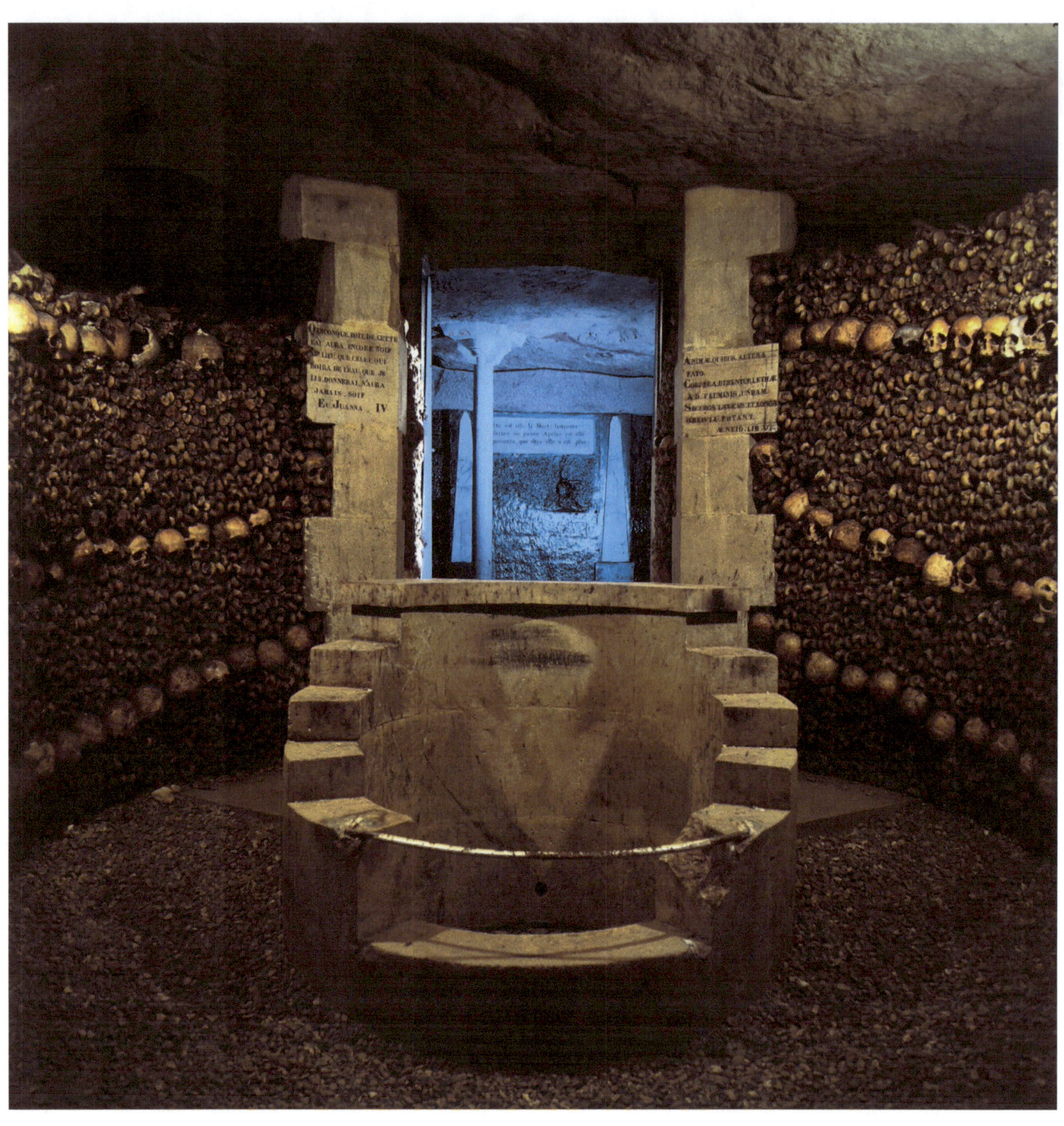

The Samaritan Woman's Fountain. A spring surrounded by a small circular space made of bones where quarrymen used to get water for their personal use. In the Gospel a woman from Samarita gave water to Jesus.

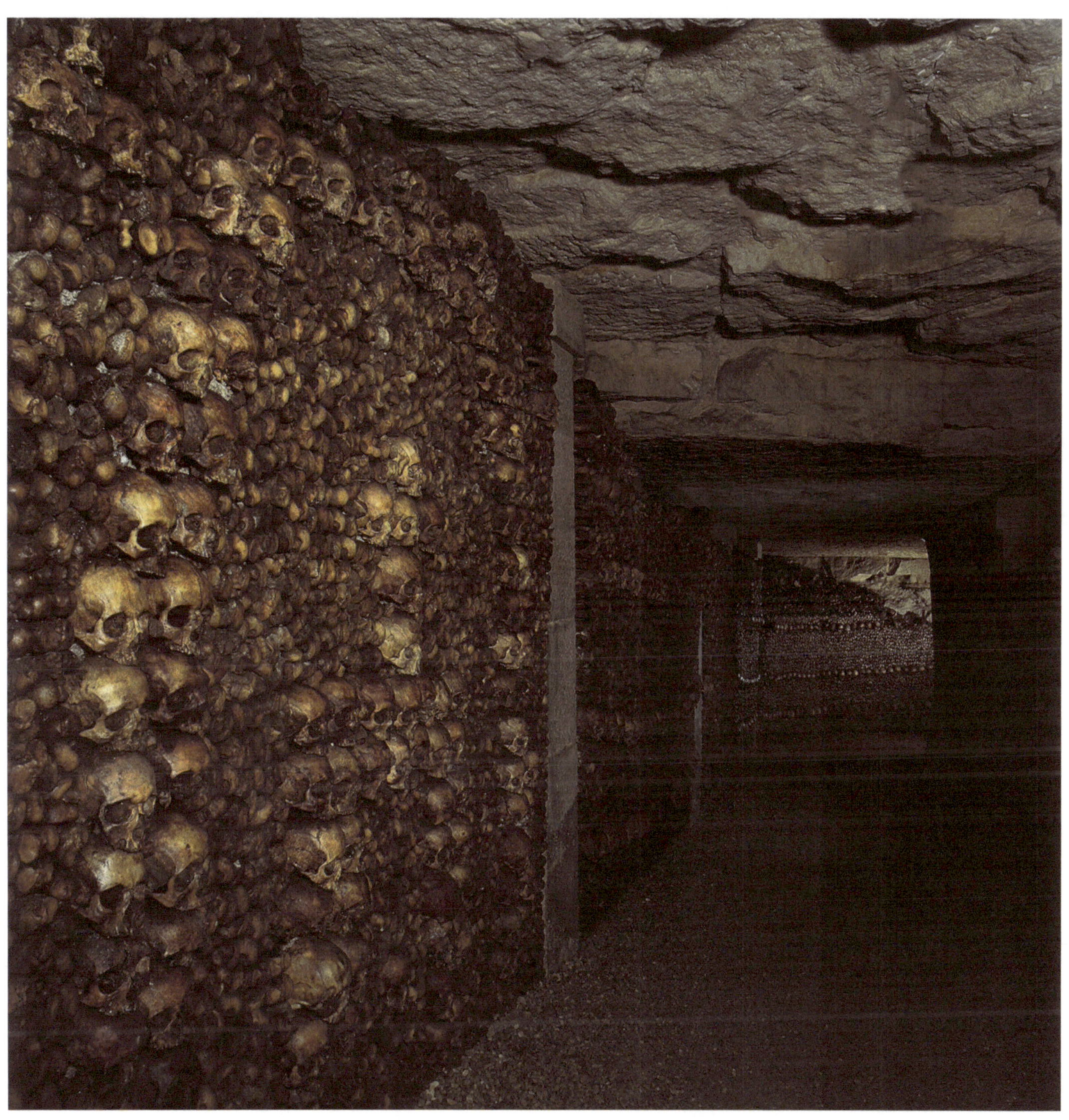

The removal of the bones began after the blessing of the place on April 7, 1786 and was continued until 1788, always at night and according to a ceremonial made up of a procession of priests who sang the burial service along the way borrowed by the tipcarts charged with bones and covered with a black veil. Until 1814, the bones of all the cemeteries of Paris were collected this way

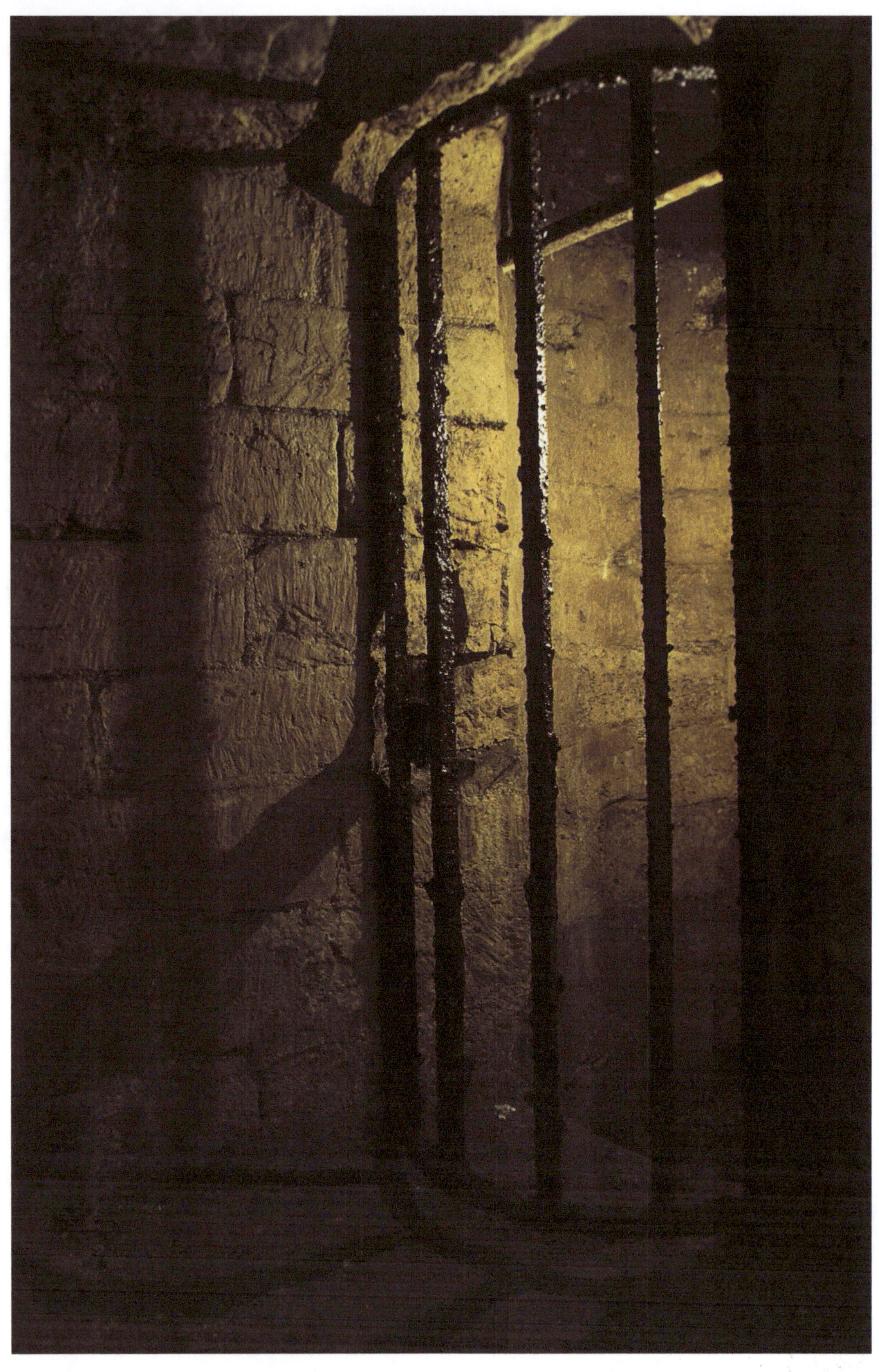

Arched door protecting a passage to a lower level

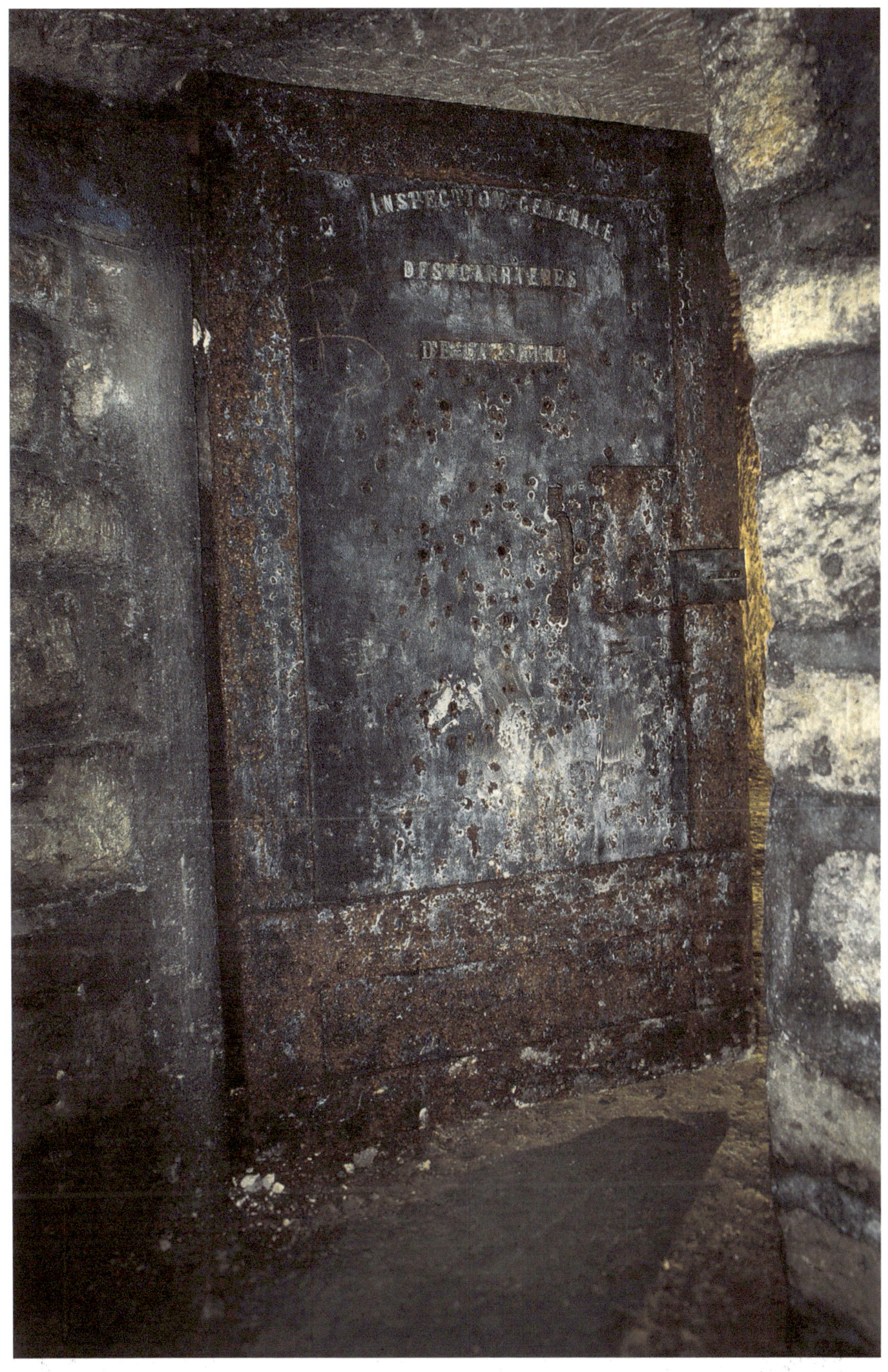

Access door to the galleries under the Reservoir of Montsouris

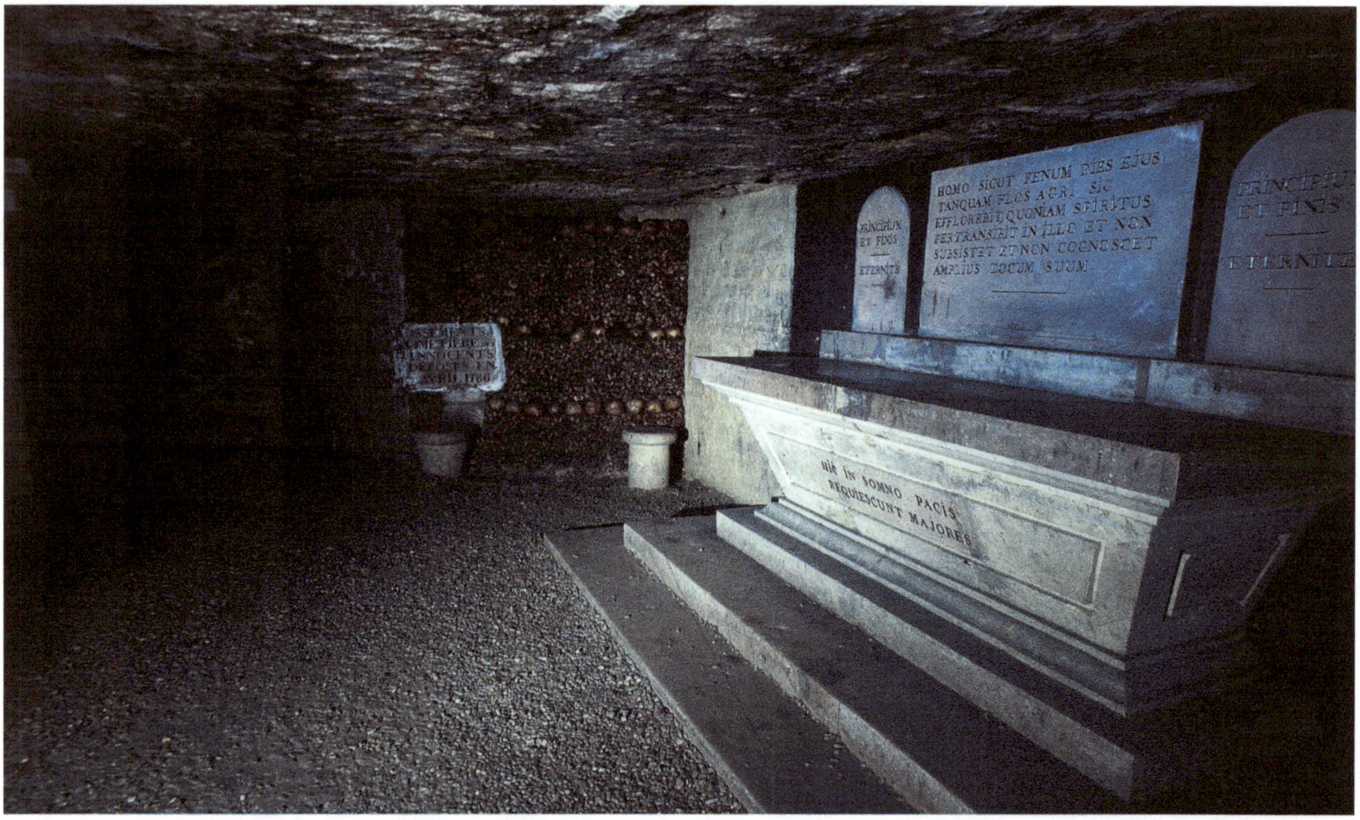

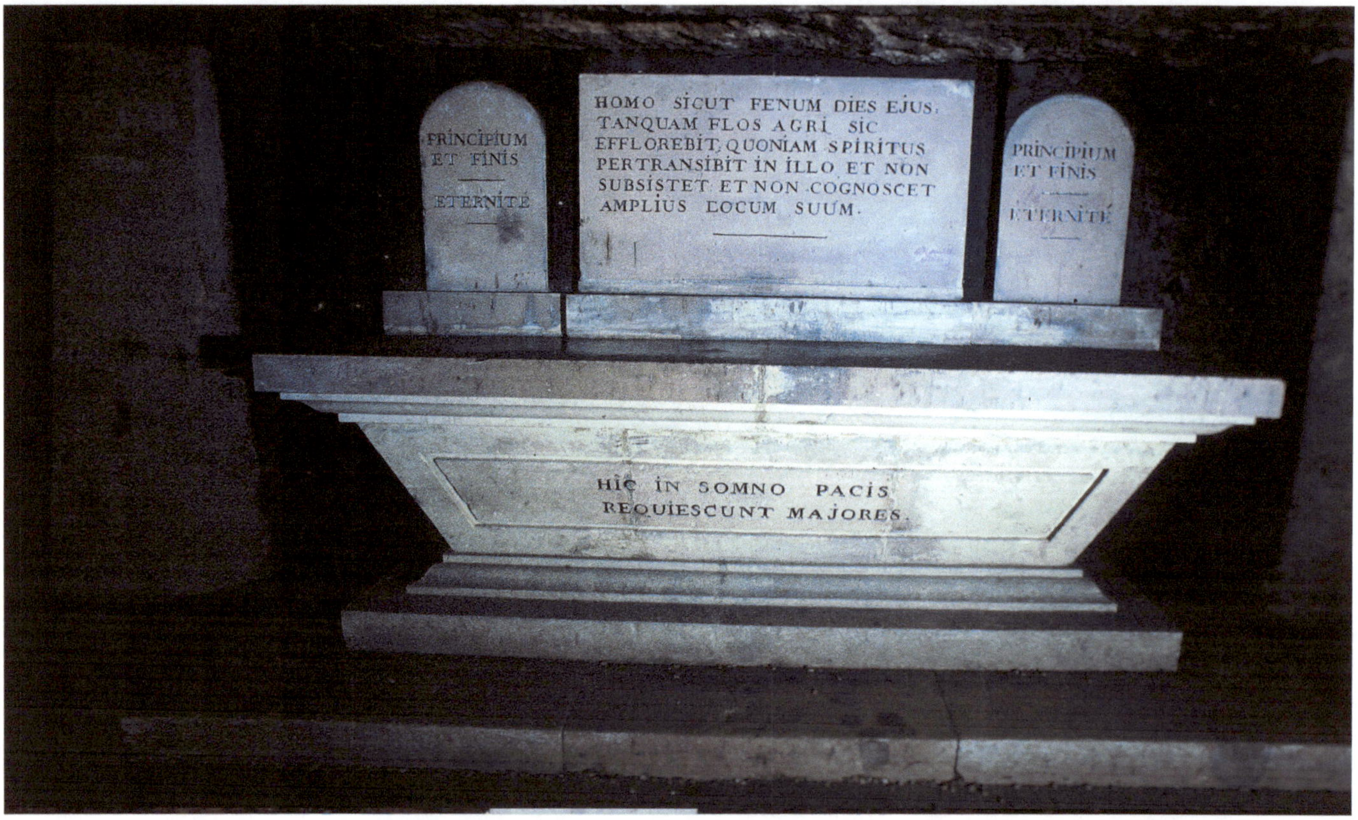

Altar dedicated to the Catacombs, situated under No 2, Alembert Street

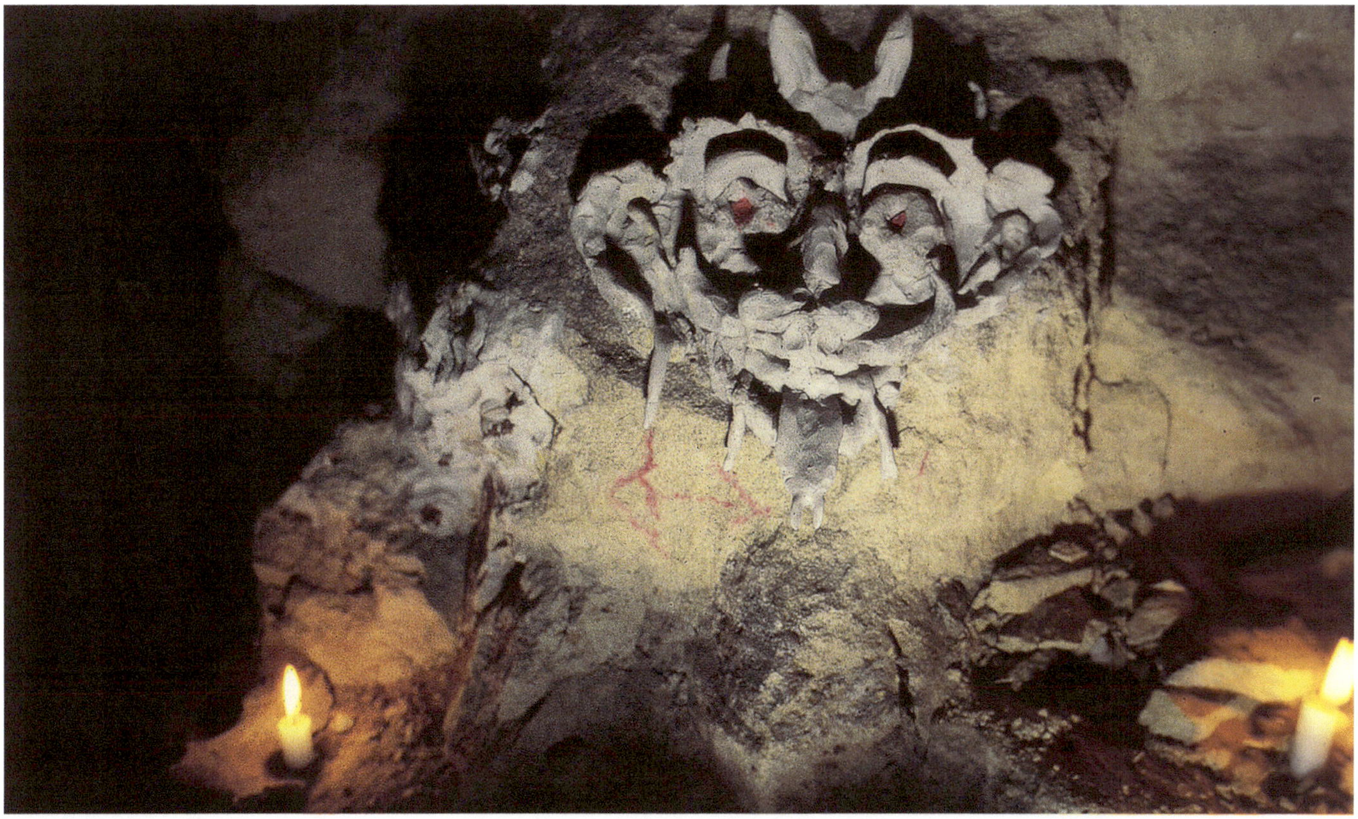

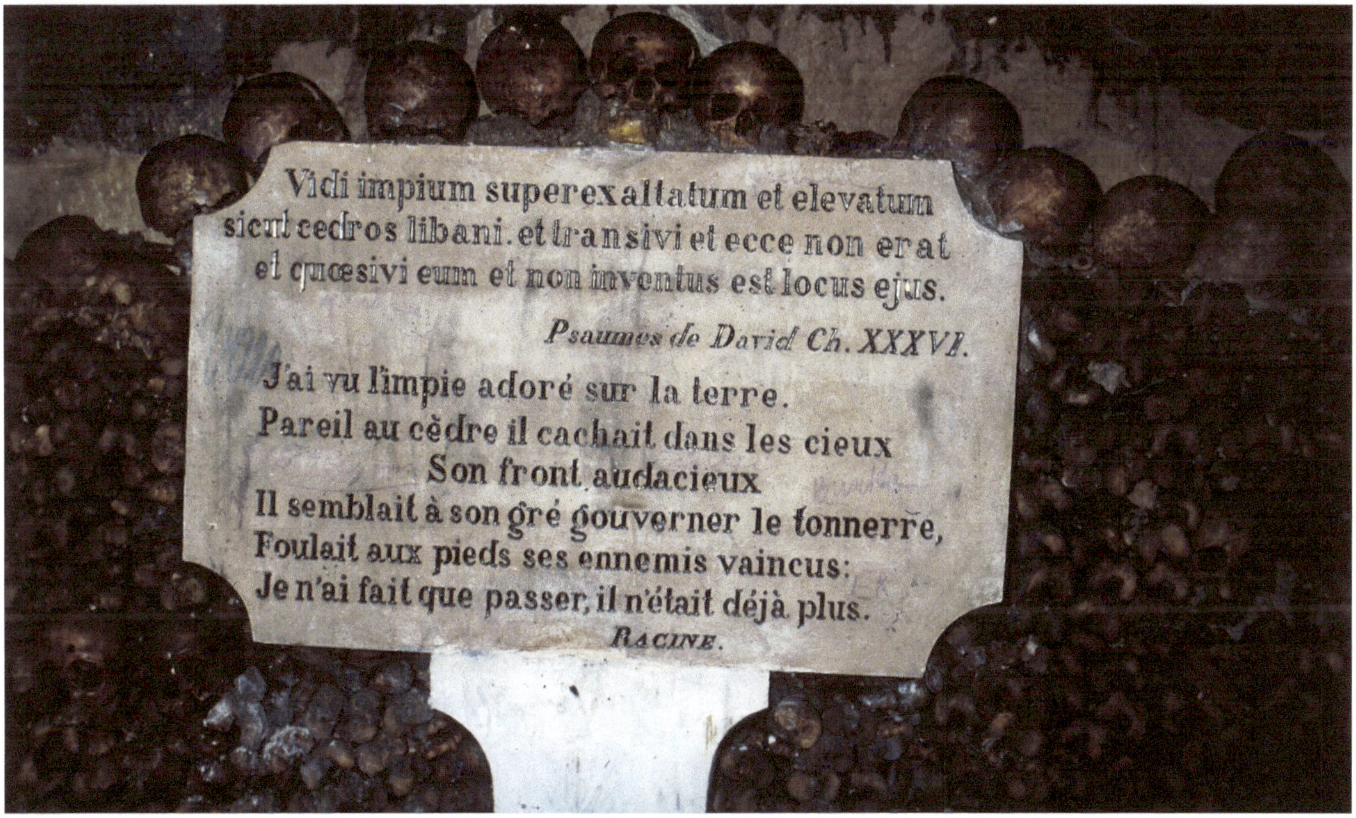

Gravestones and funerary monuments

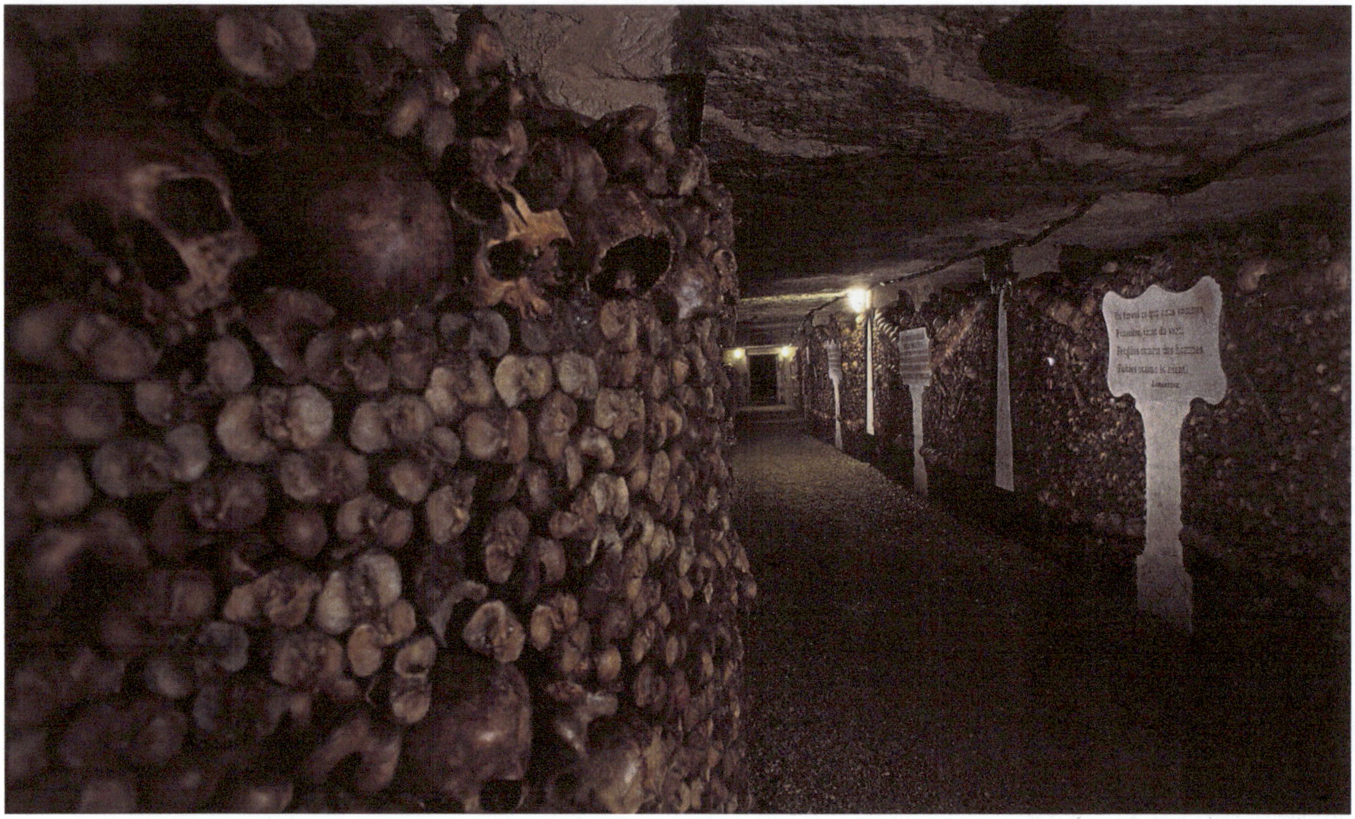

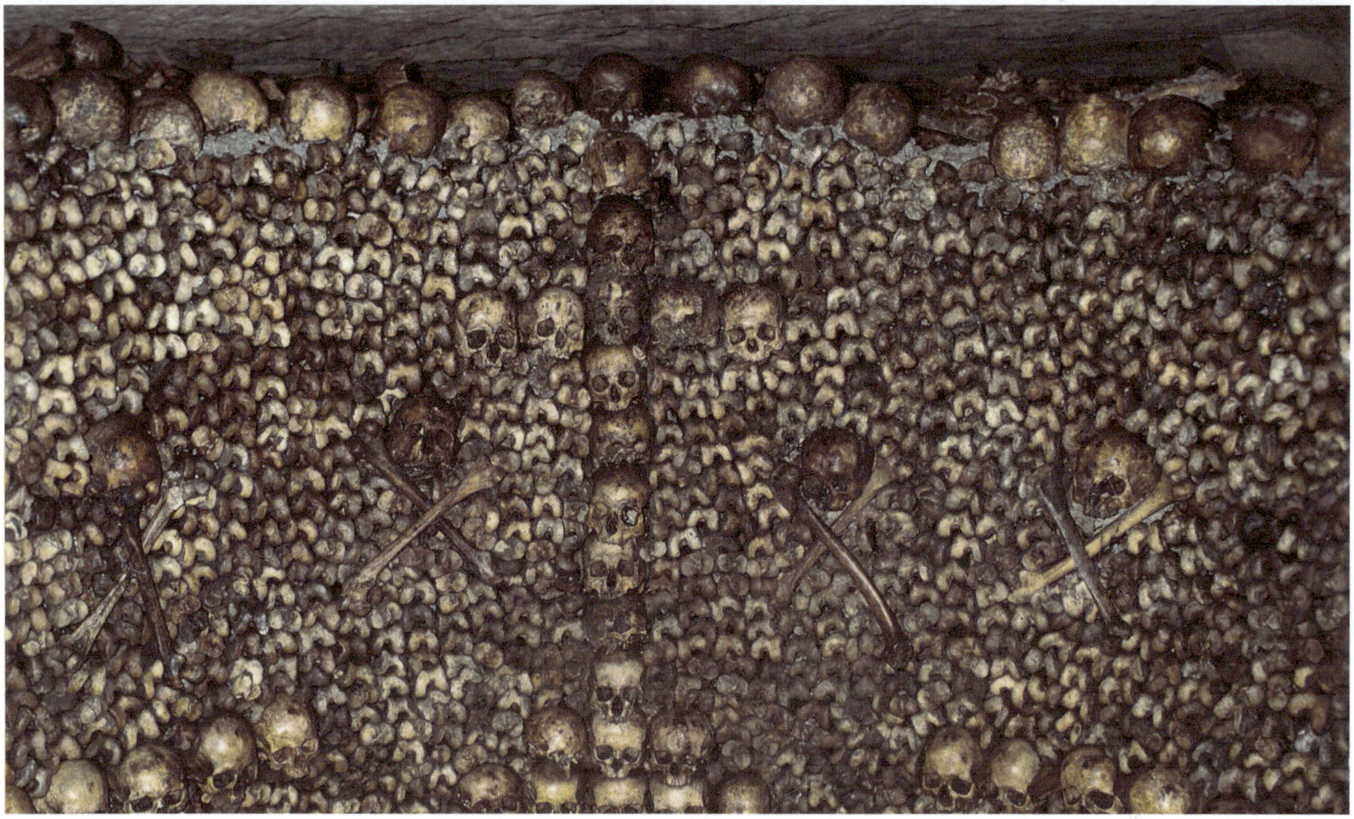

6 millions of Parisian Skulls

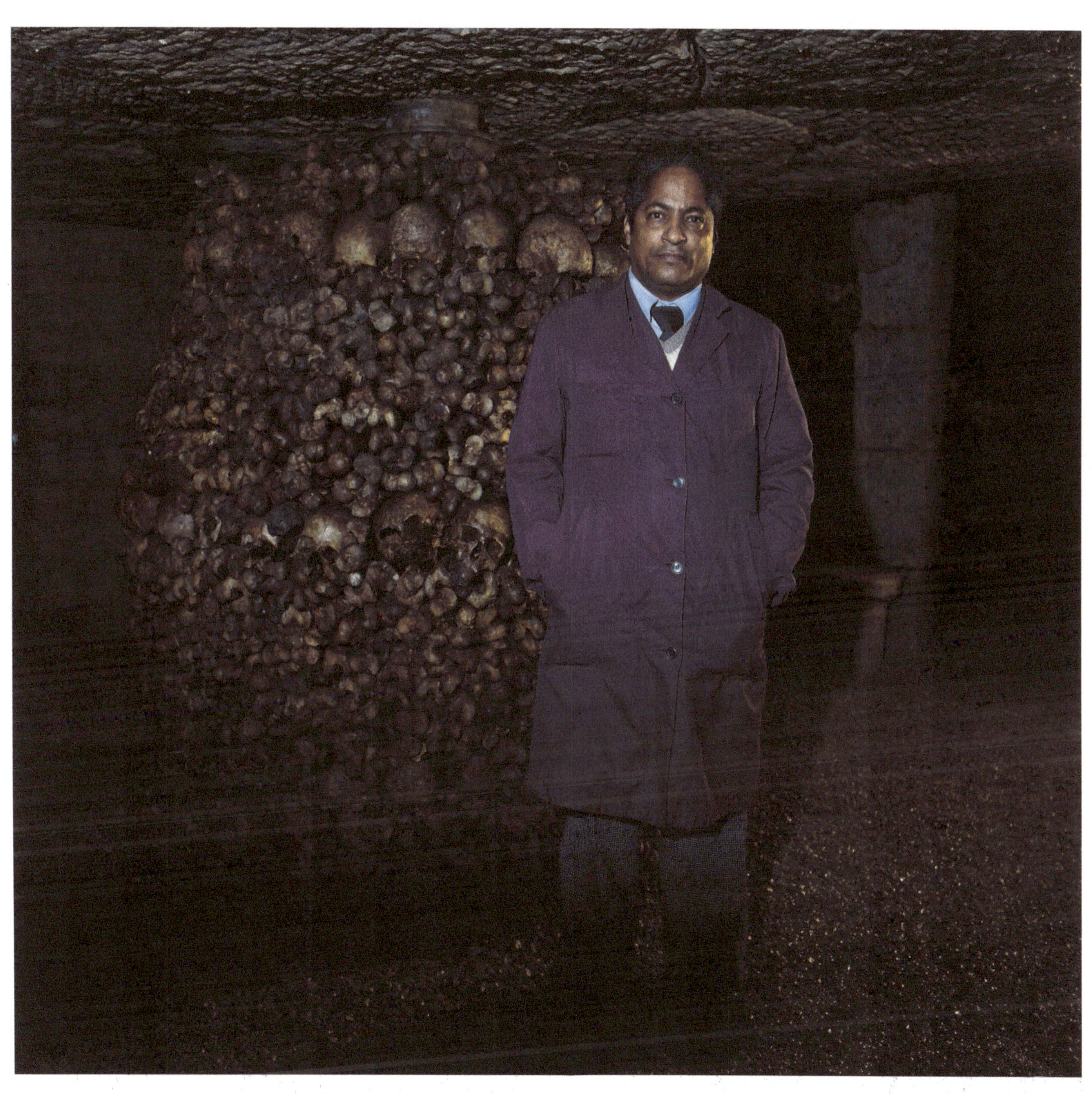

Man in charge of the Catacombs

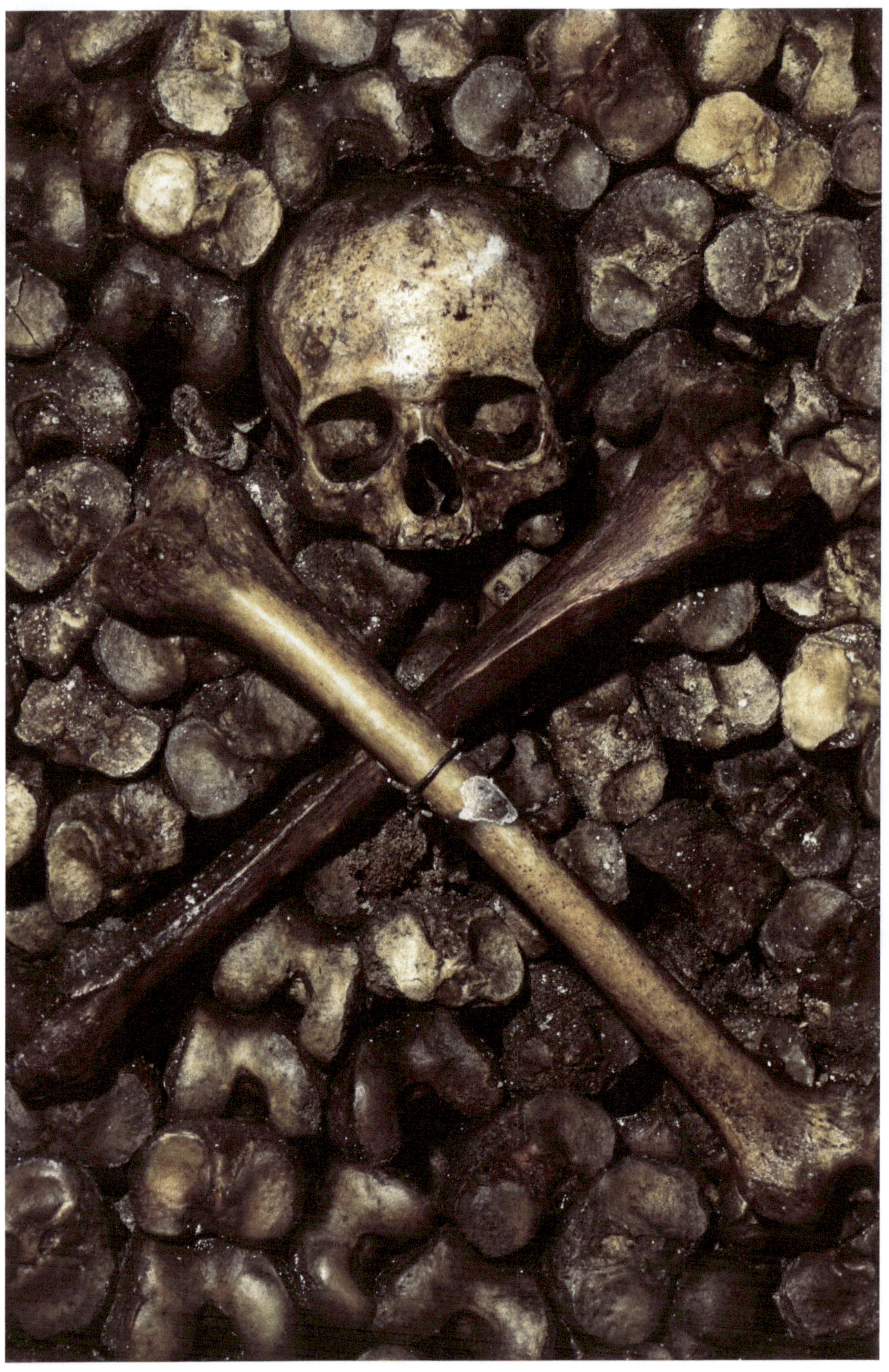

Pirate like design...

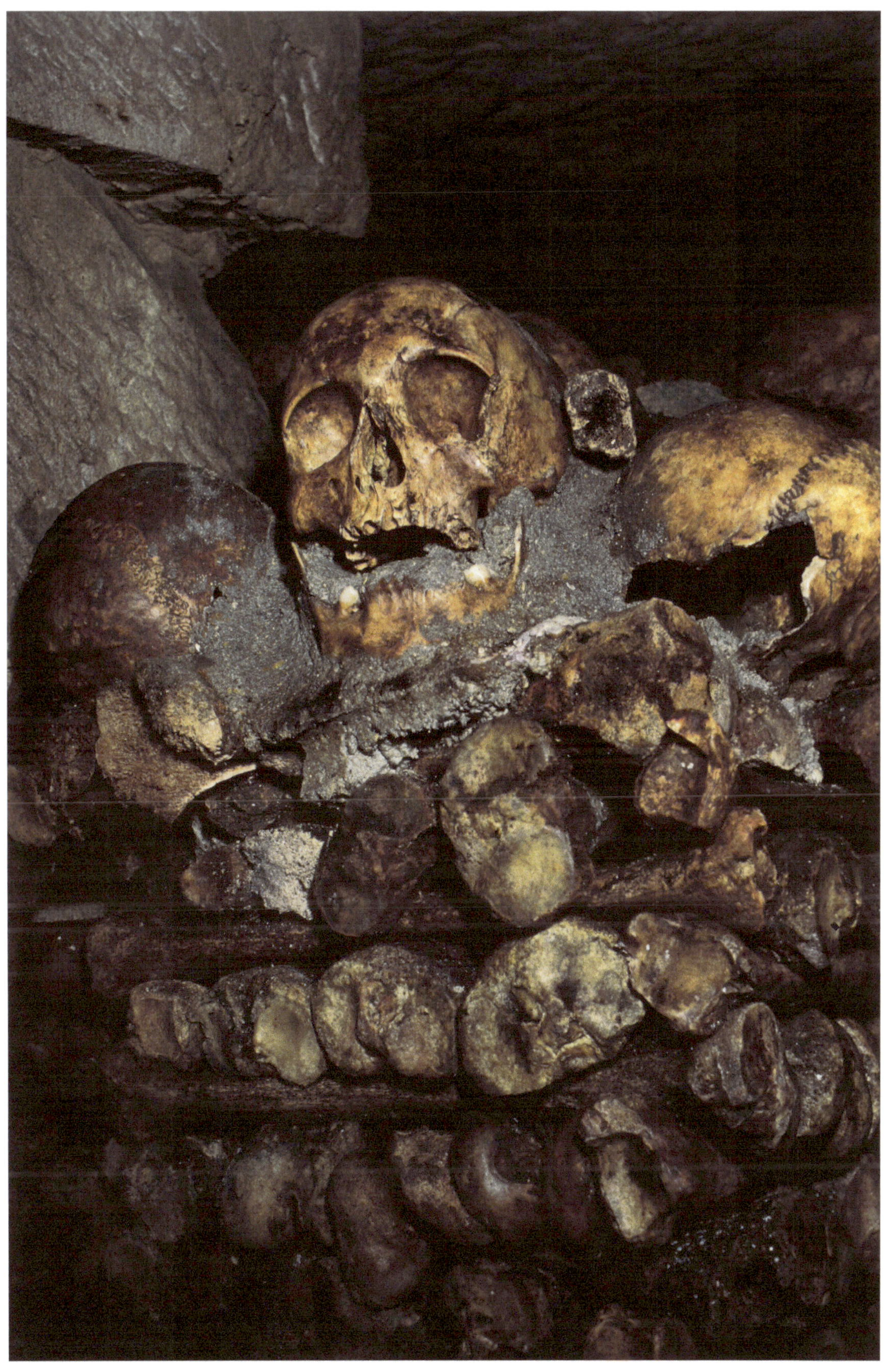

Bonded for eternity

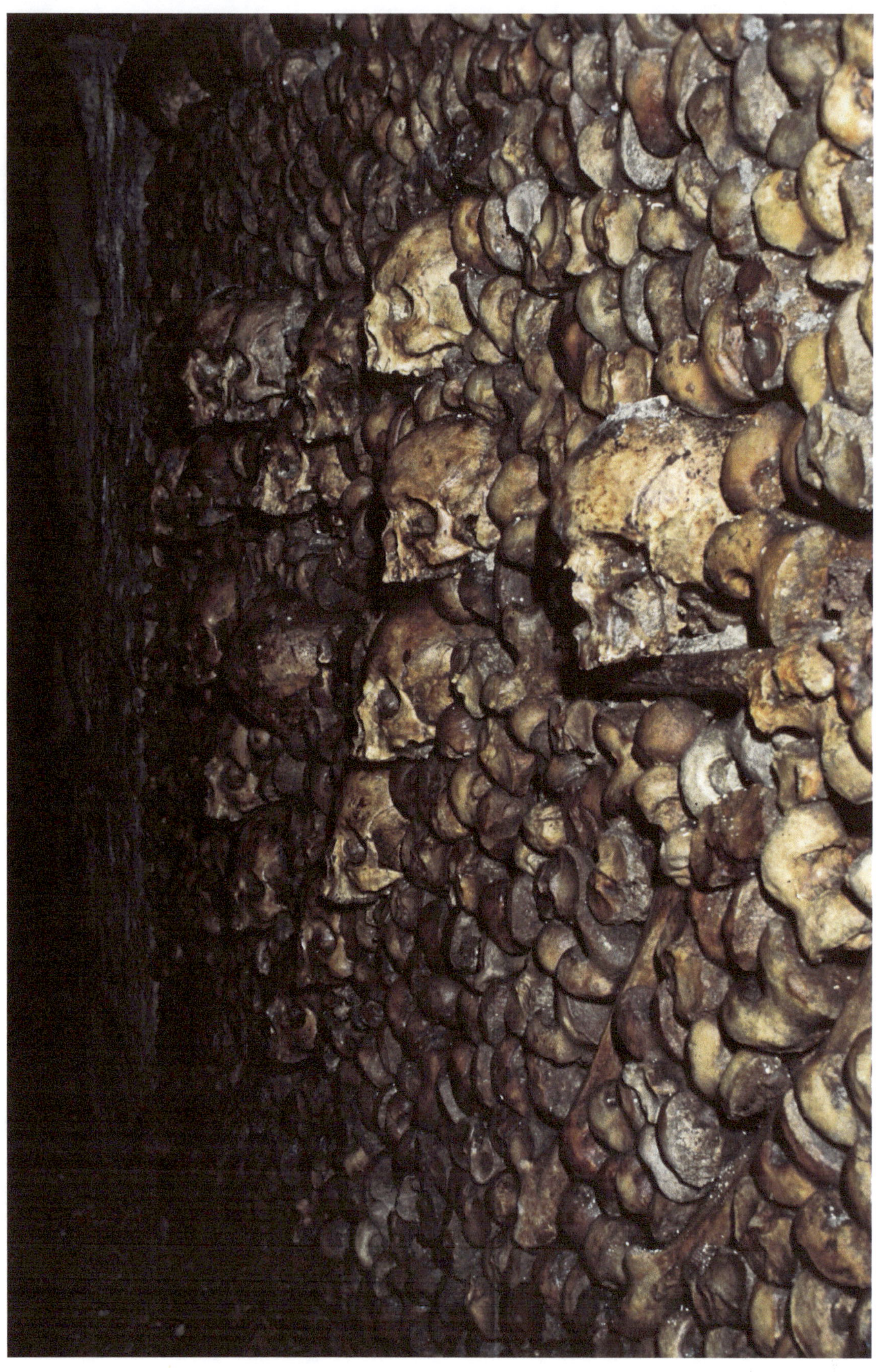

Wall of skulls, 10 feet deep

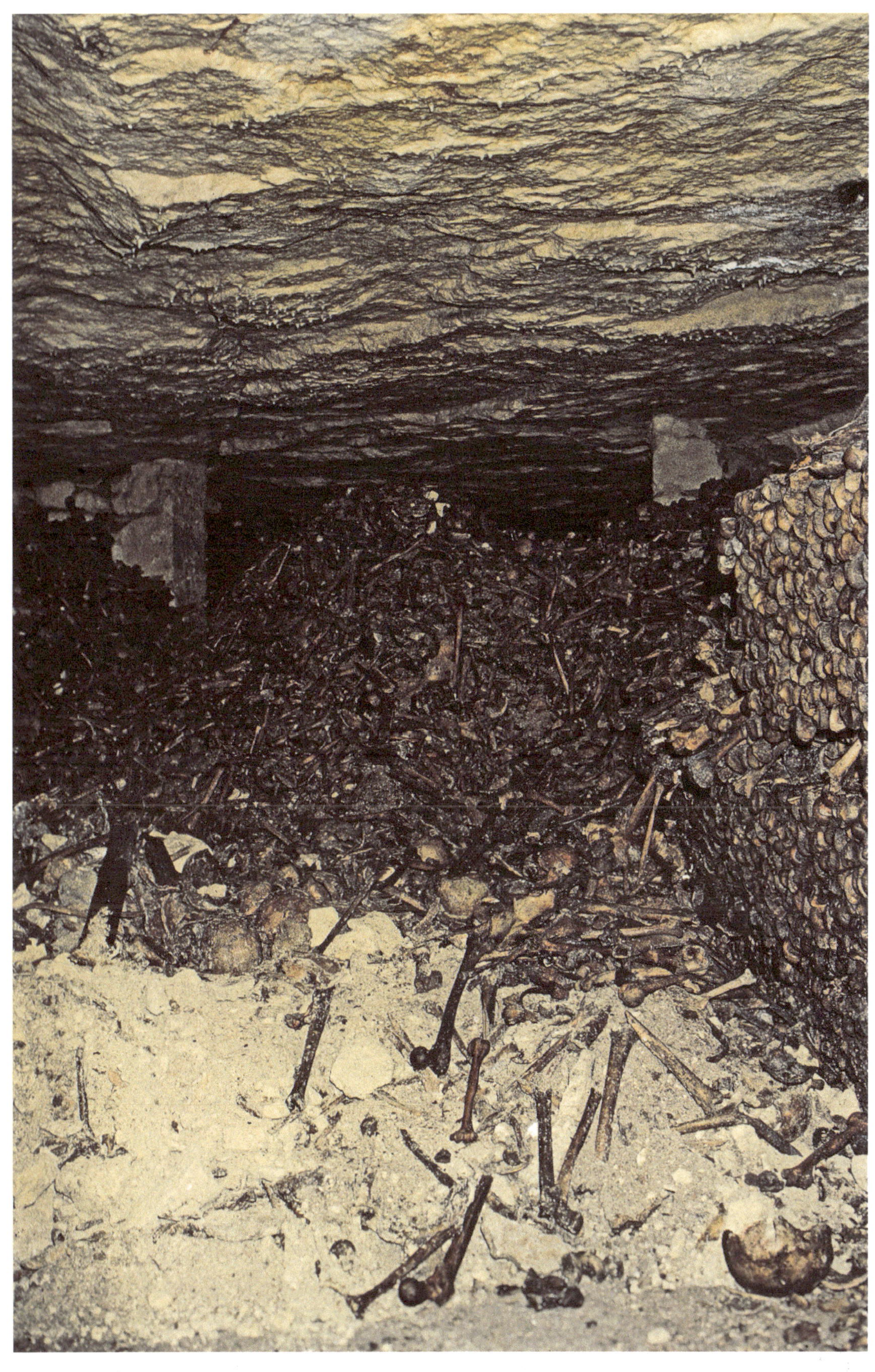

End of the Catacombs. The pile of bones goes deep into the quarry

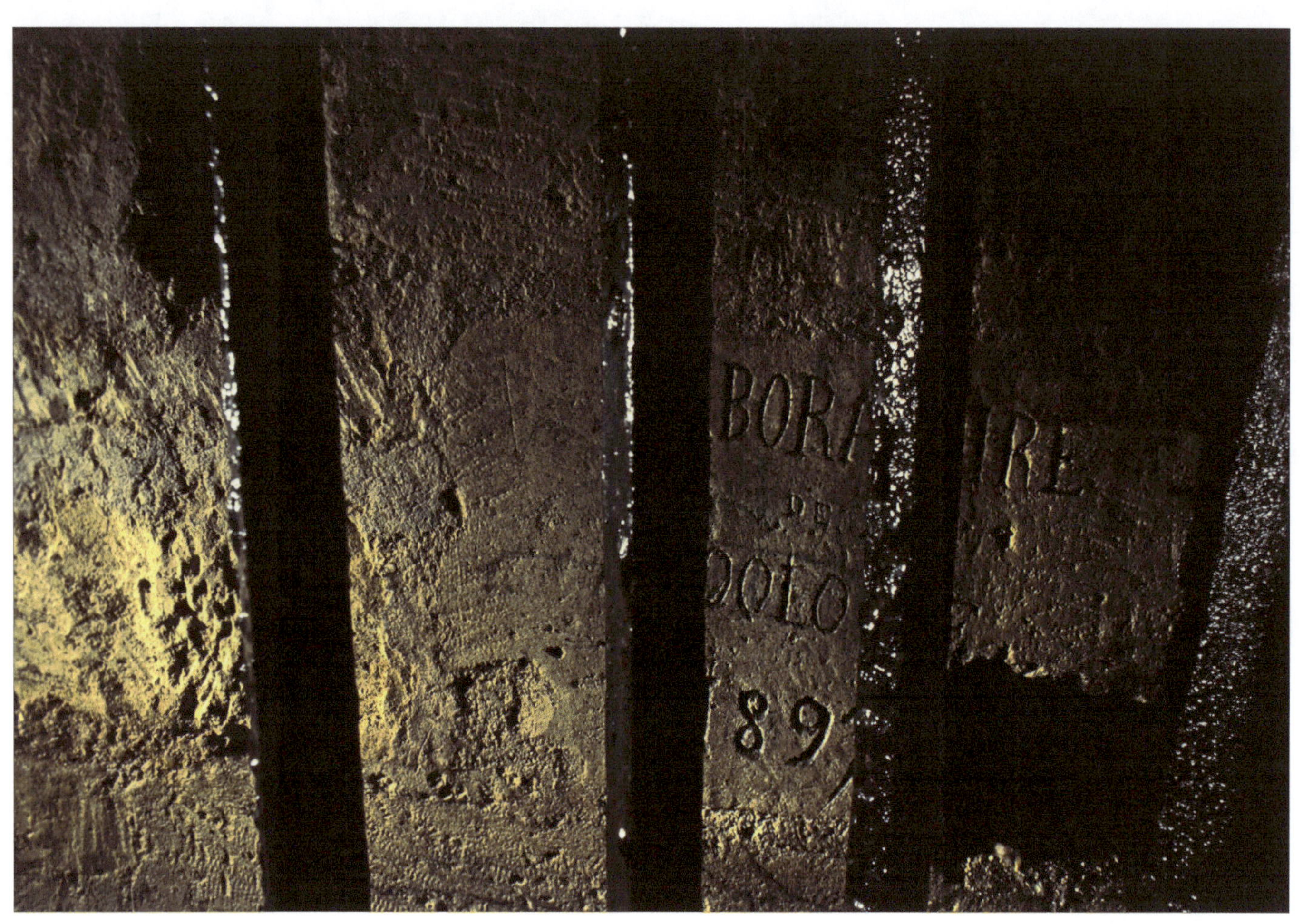

Dead End.

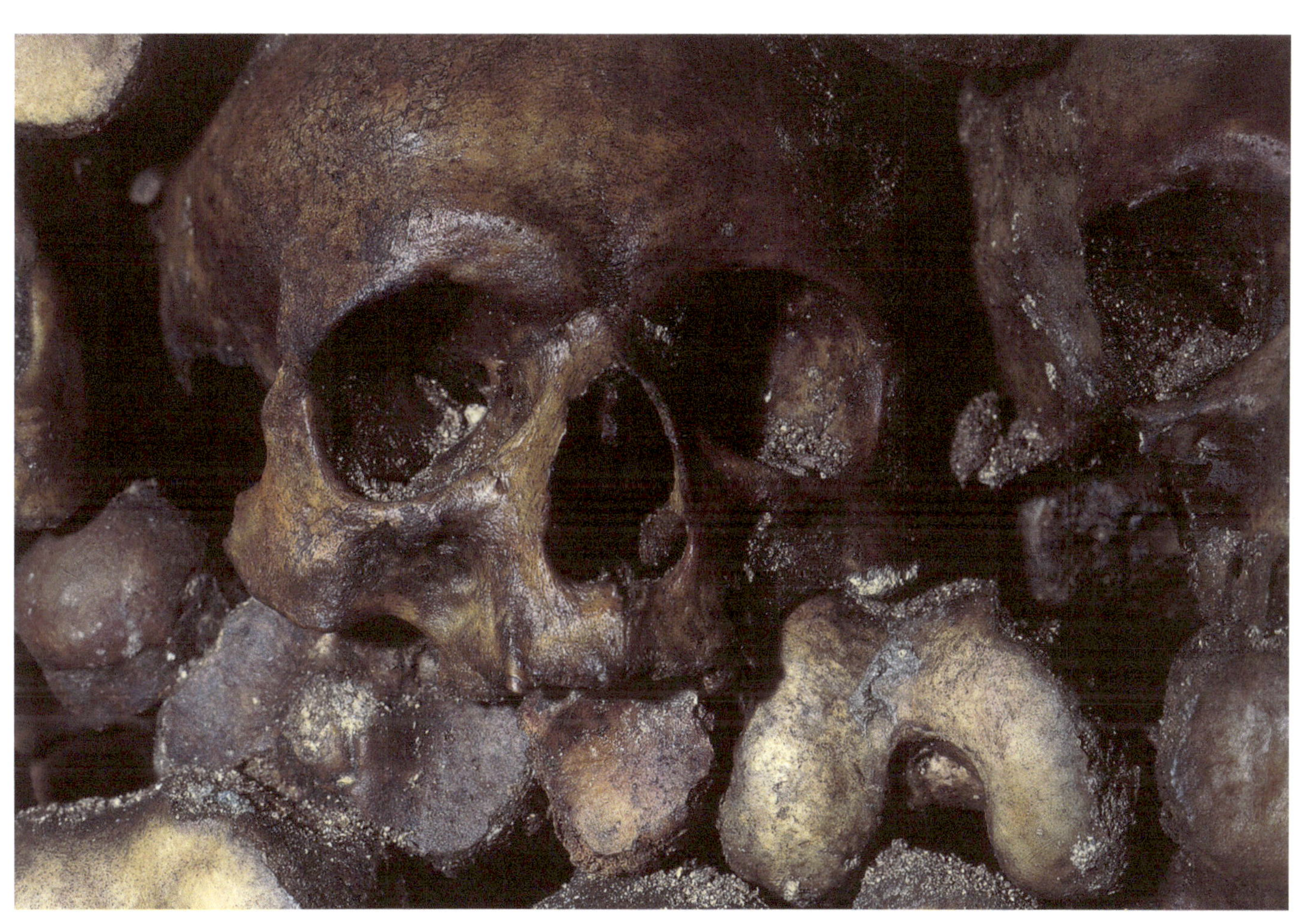

Skull and bones

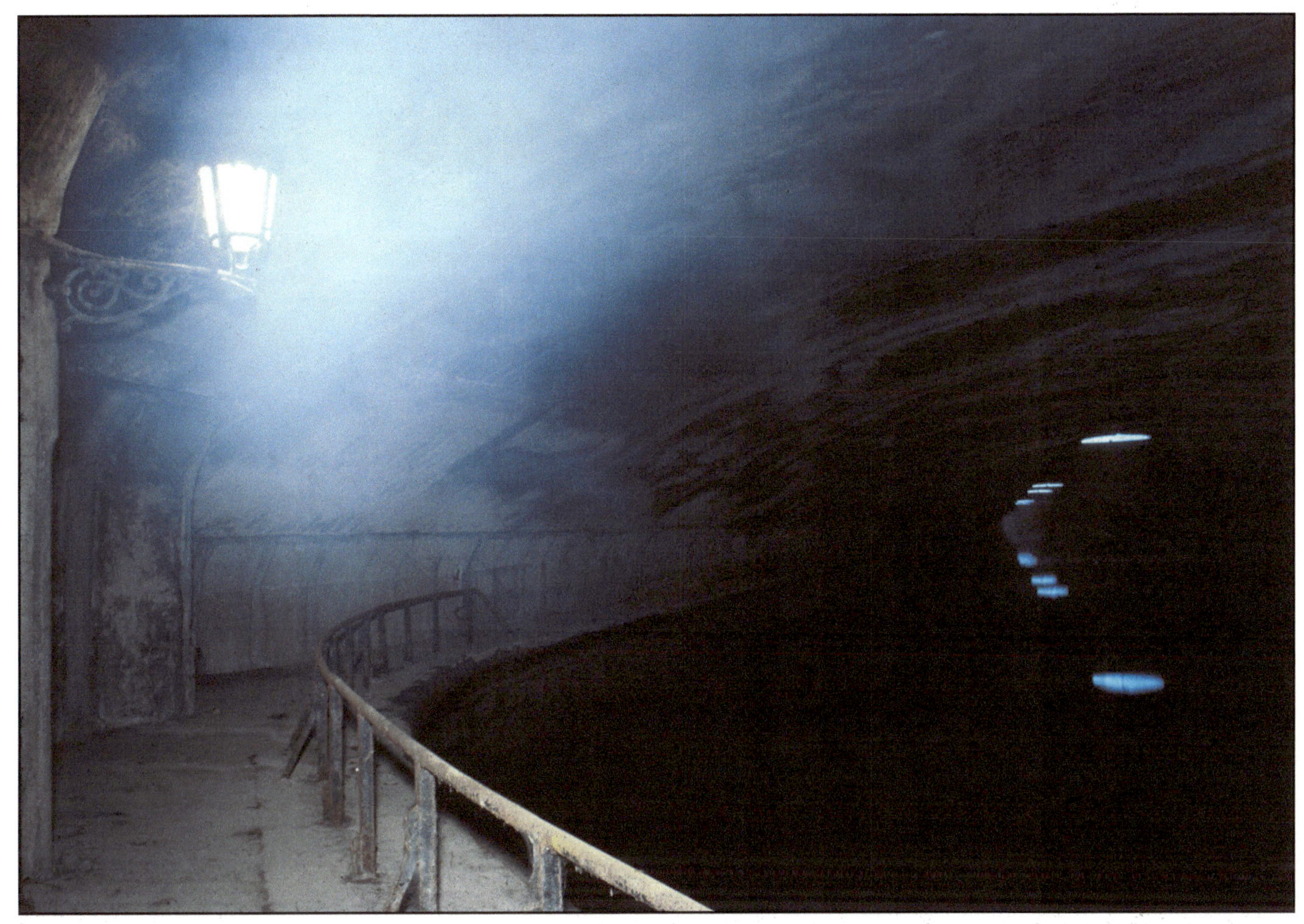

CHAPTER THREE: THE CANAL SAINT-MARTIN

The canal Saint Martin was built in 1825 to link the La Villette Bassin to the Seine River. It was covered in 1860 on a 2,5 miles. Section From La Bastille to La Republique. The official reason was to facilitate traffic in a crowded area. In reality, the canal was a protection, a barrier used by traditionally revolutionary neighborhood such as Menilmontant and the Faubourg Montmartre. Once covered it was easy for the cavalry to deploy and maintain order.

Only 15 barges use the canal daily.

The access to the underground canal is forbidden. In fact it is quite easy to jump over the metal door when the lockmaster in charge of the waterway is not watching.

It is a magical promenade…

Canal entrance

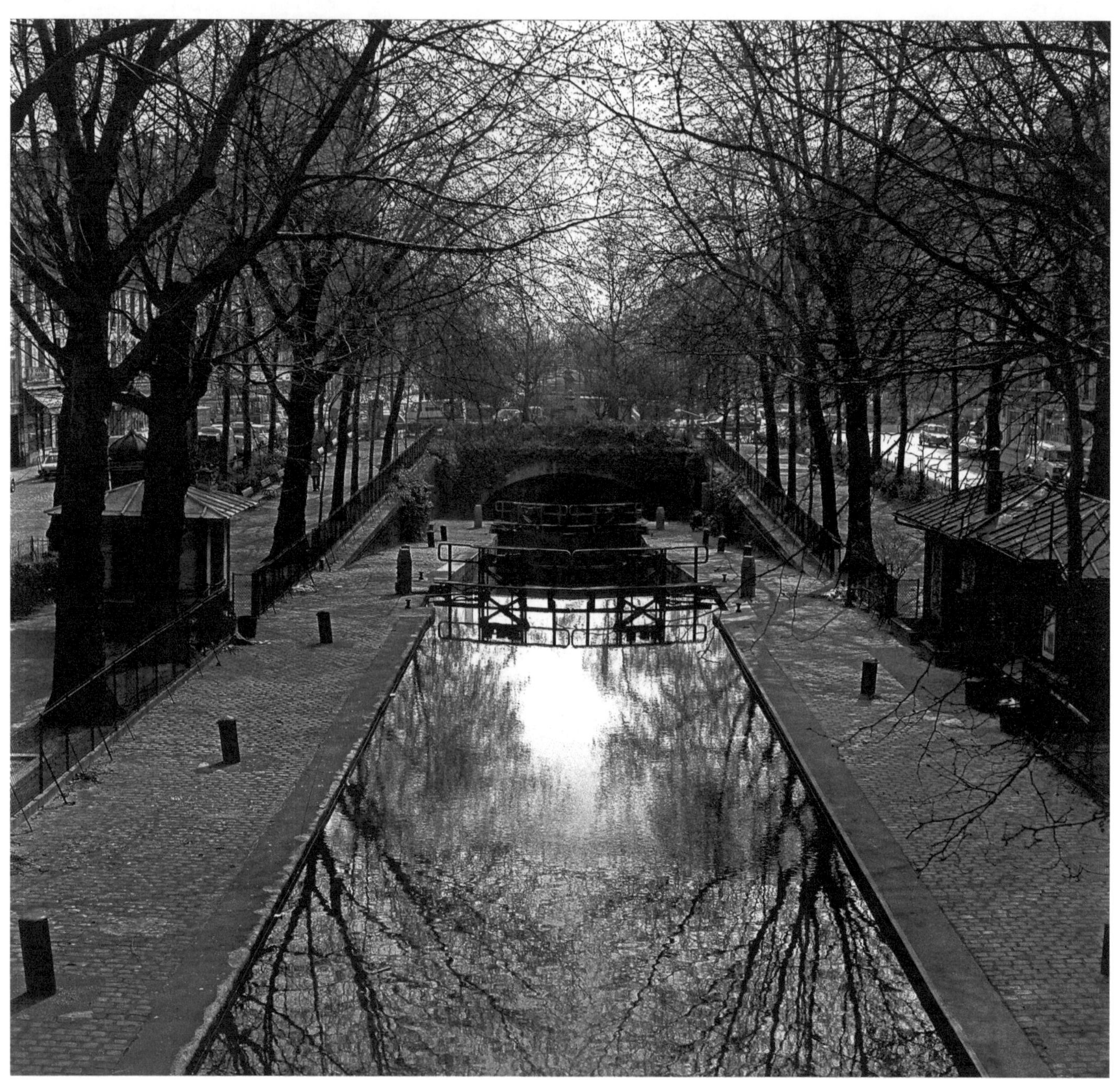

Entrance at the Richard Lenoir Blvd

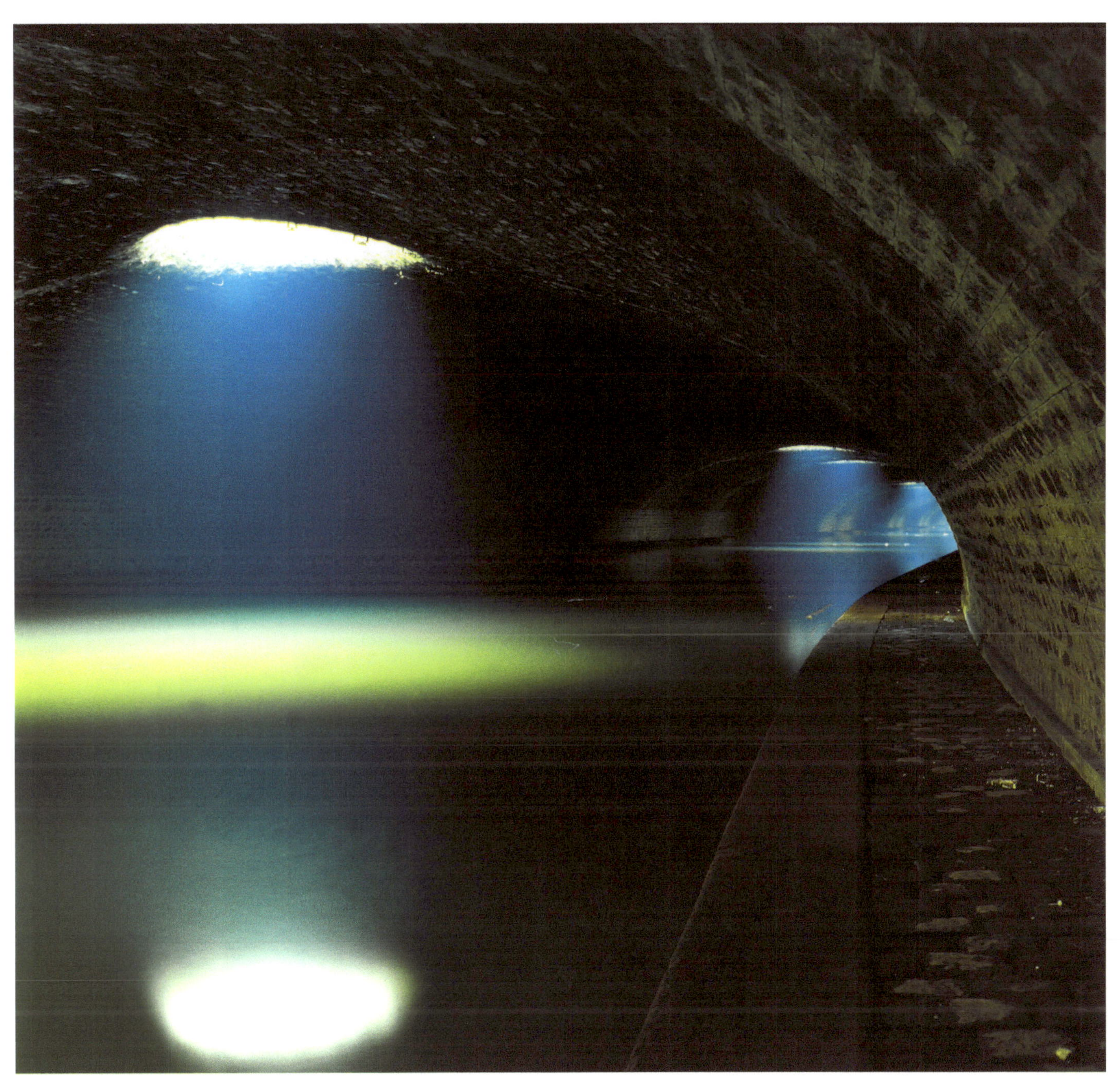

Magical beams of light shine through the ventilation hole and reflect on the water

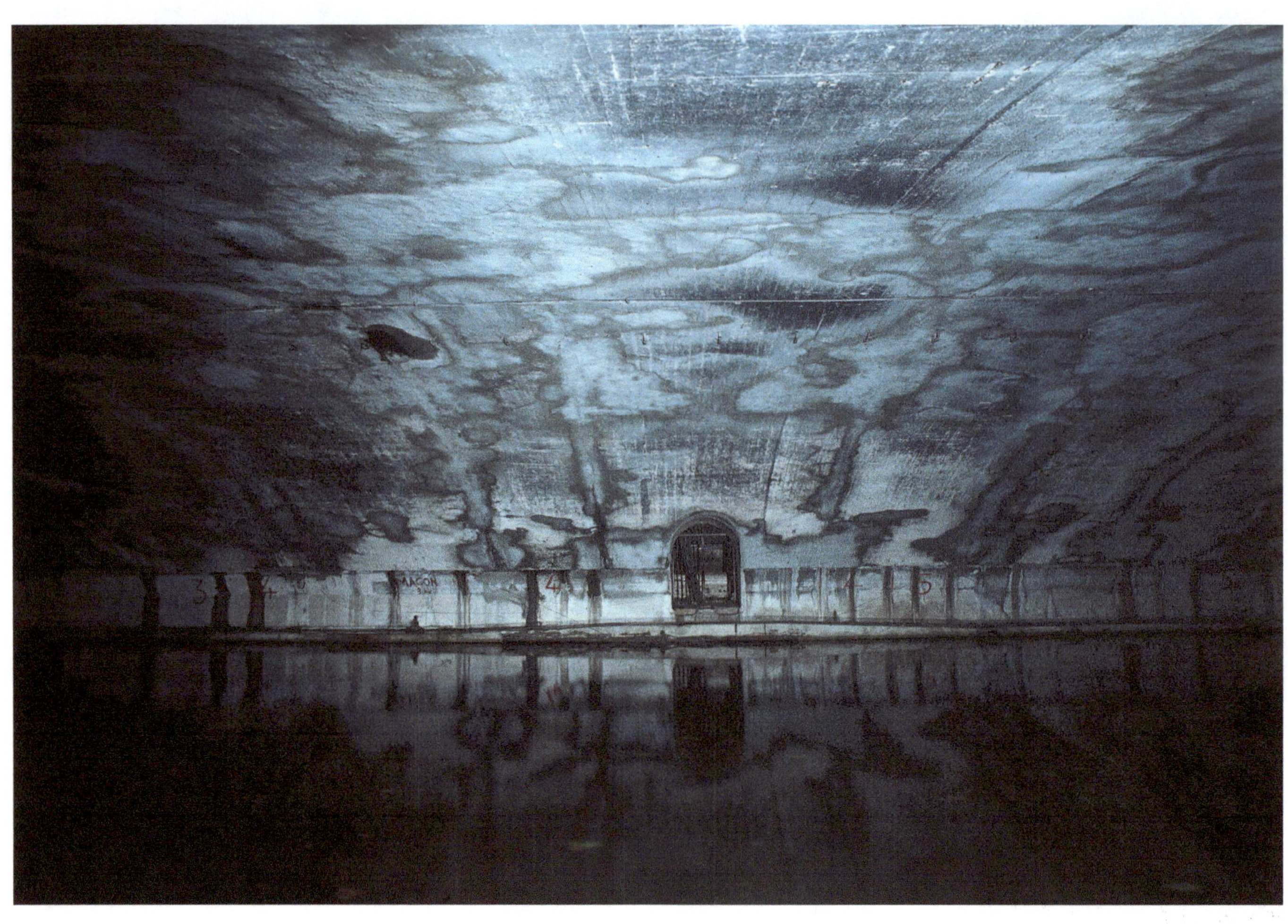

Door leading to the sewers

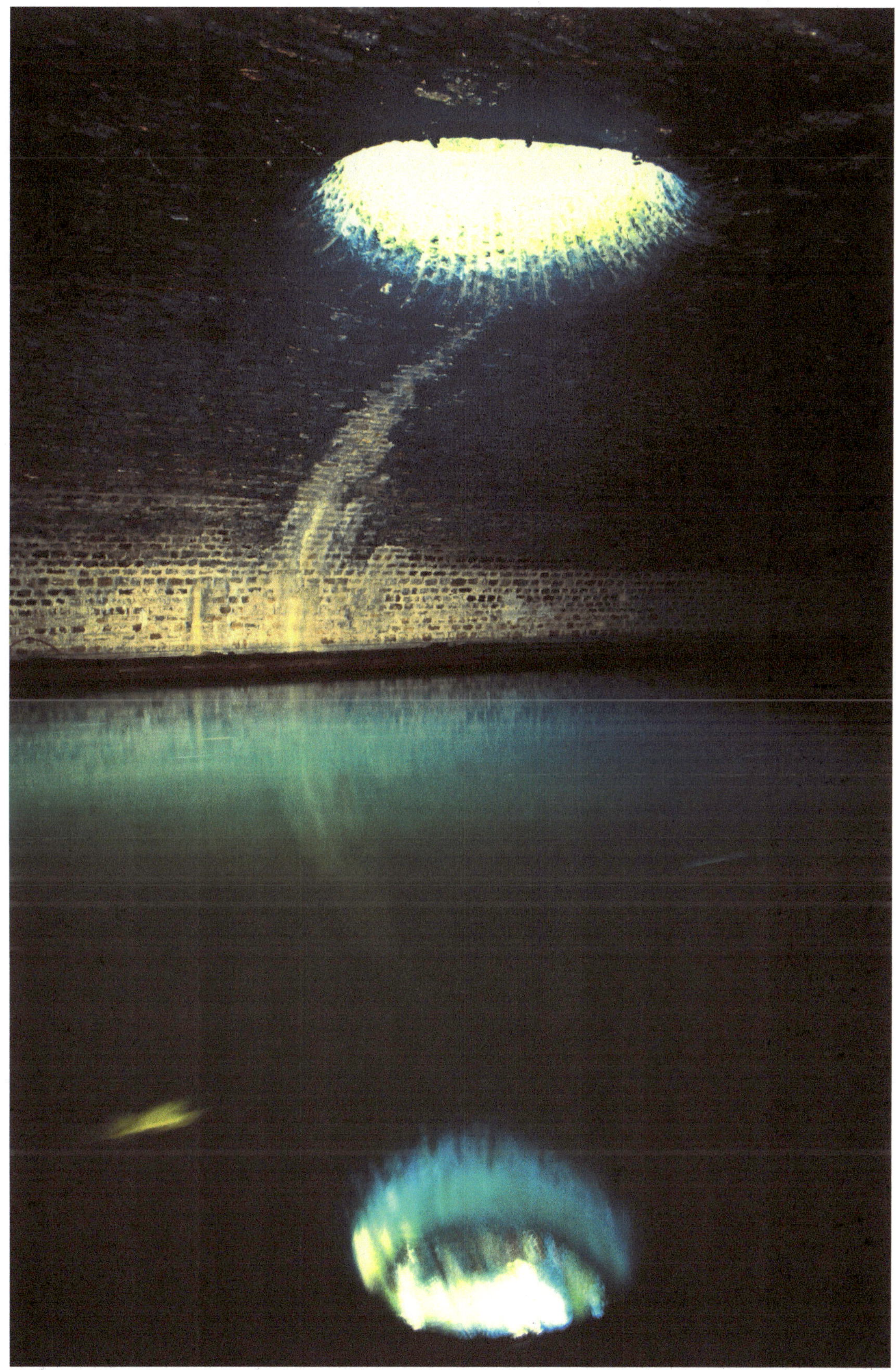

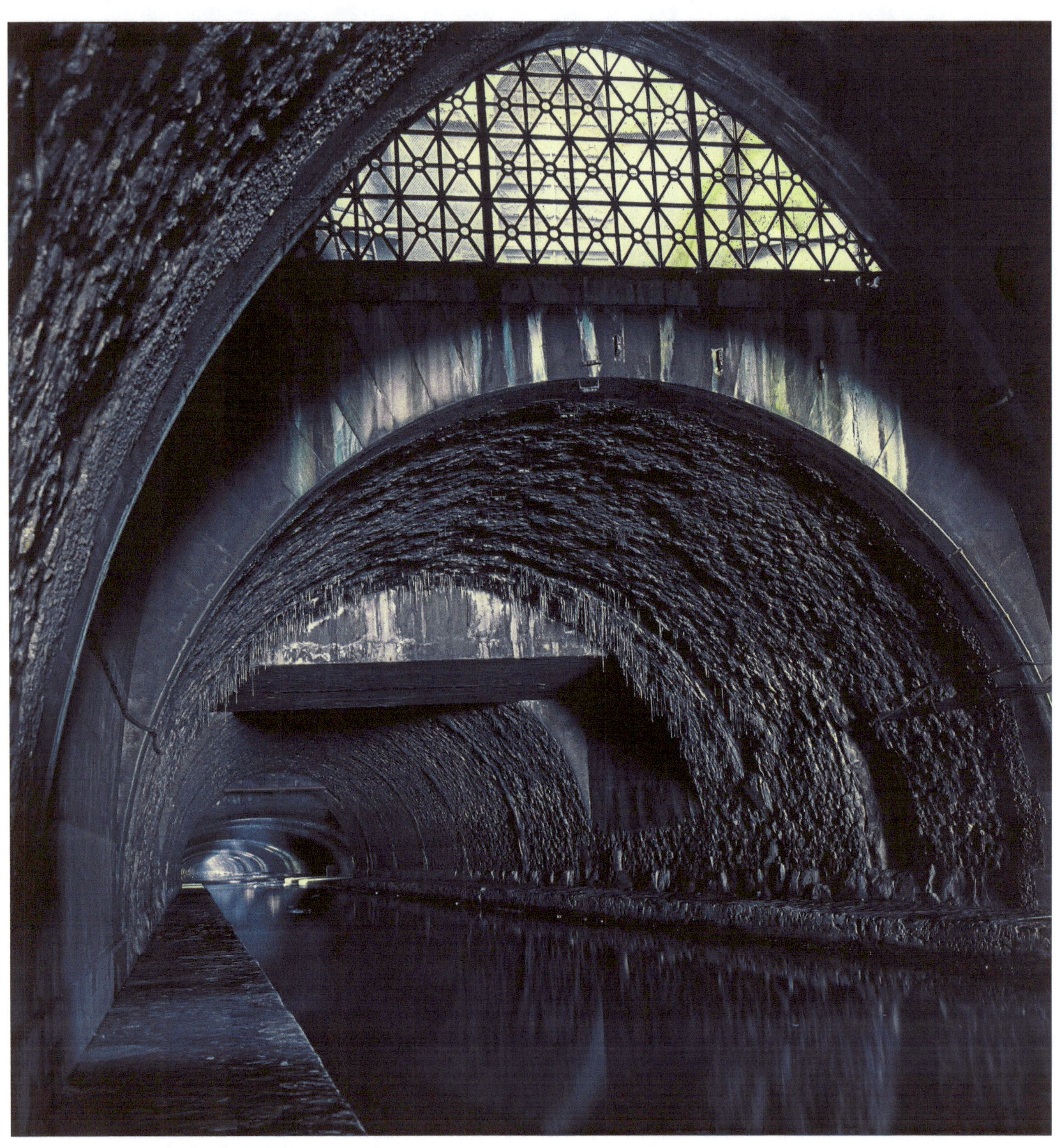

The Canal Saint Martin runs under The Colonne de Juillet (July Column) a monument to the Revolution of 1830. It stands in the center of the Place de la Bastille. There is a secret passage from the canal to the column. I took it once and discovered a room full of Egyptians sarcophagus stored there because of lack of space at the Louvre Museum

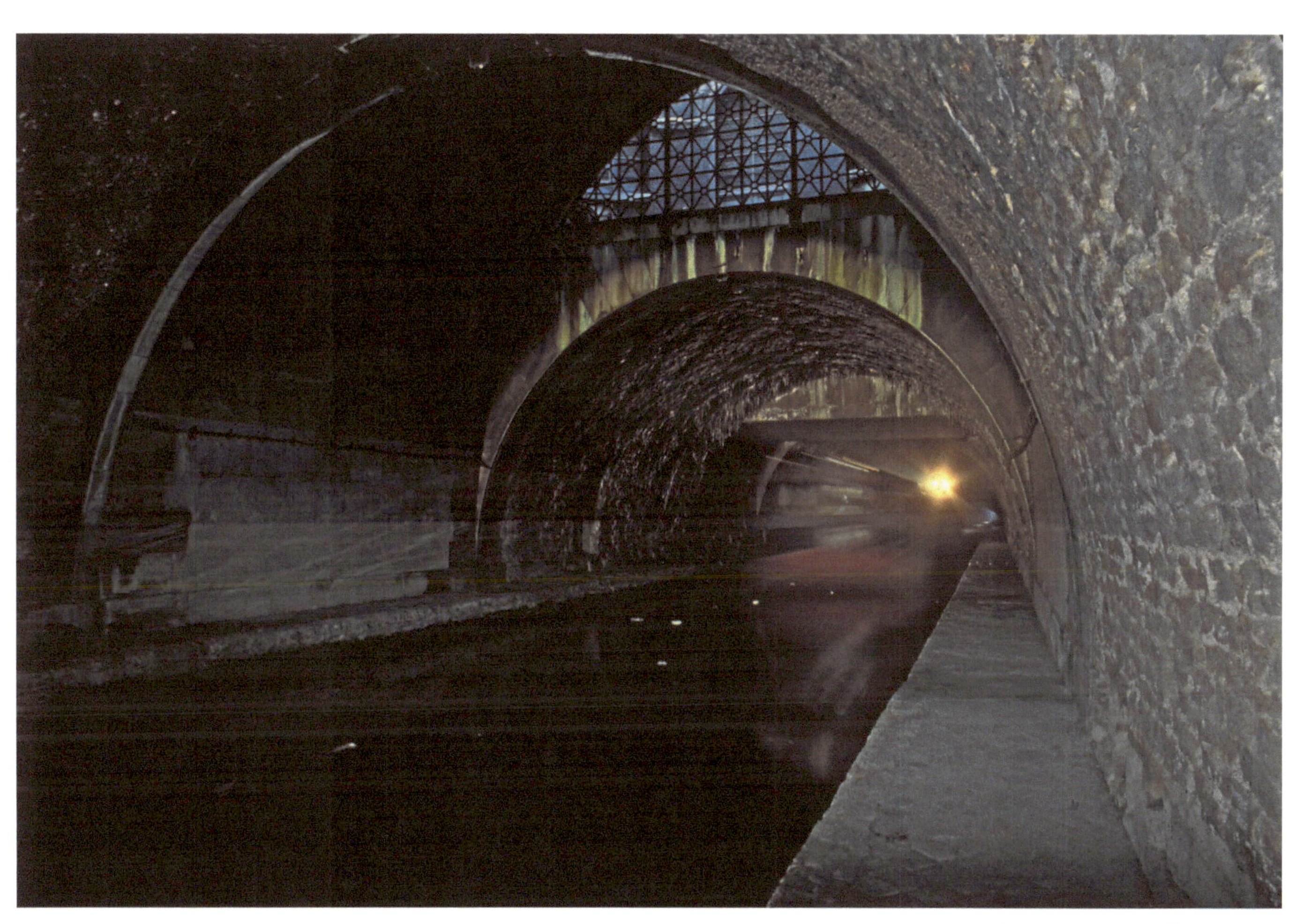

Barge exits from the underground canal into the Arsenal Bassin connected to the Seine River

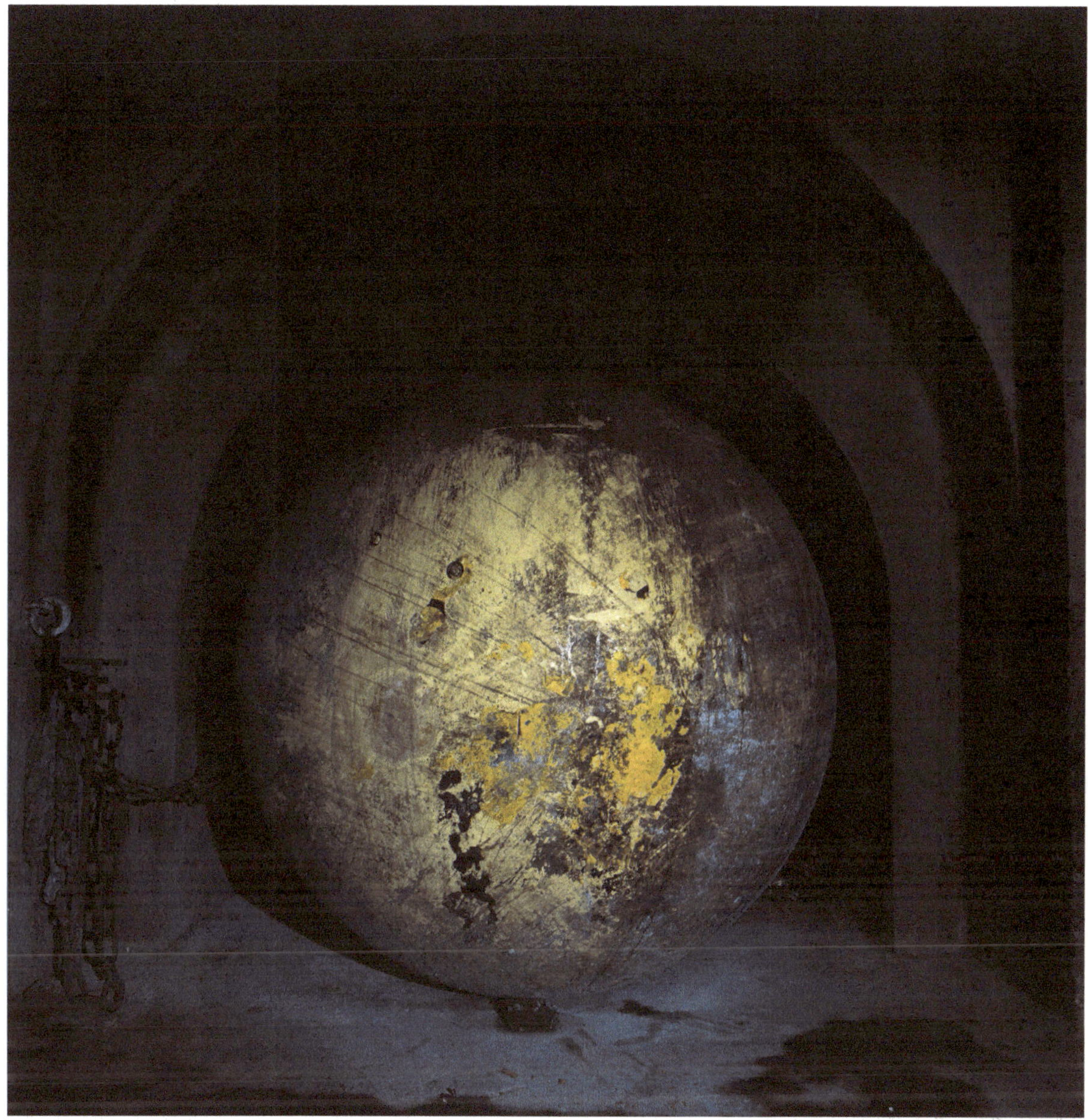

CHAPTER FOUR: THE SEWERS

Until the XVII century the Paris 'sewers were in open air, flowing straight into the Seine River. Today the network is 1,300 miles long, and the water is treated in purification plants.

The metal ball weights 1,5 ton for 10 feet high. When a tunnel is clogged up, the ball is thrown into the tunnel and floats with the current to the place where the debris obstruct the sewer flow. Of course it gets stuck. After a while, the current behind the ball raises the water level and at some point applies enough pressure on the metal sphere that it pushes the debris away. The ball rolls for several miles and reaches the end at the purification plan, pushing and crushing everything on its passage. The ball is brought back by truck to the starting point. It sounds low-tech but the technique has been workind just fine for centuries...

Cleaning metal ball

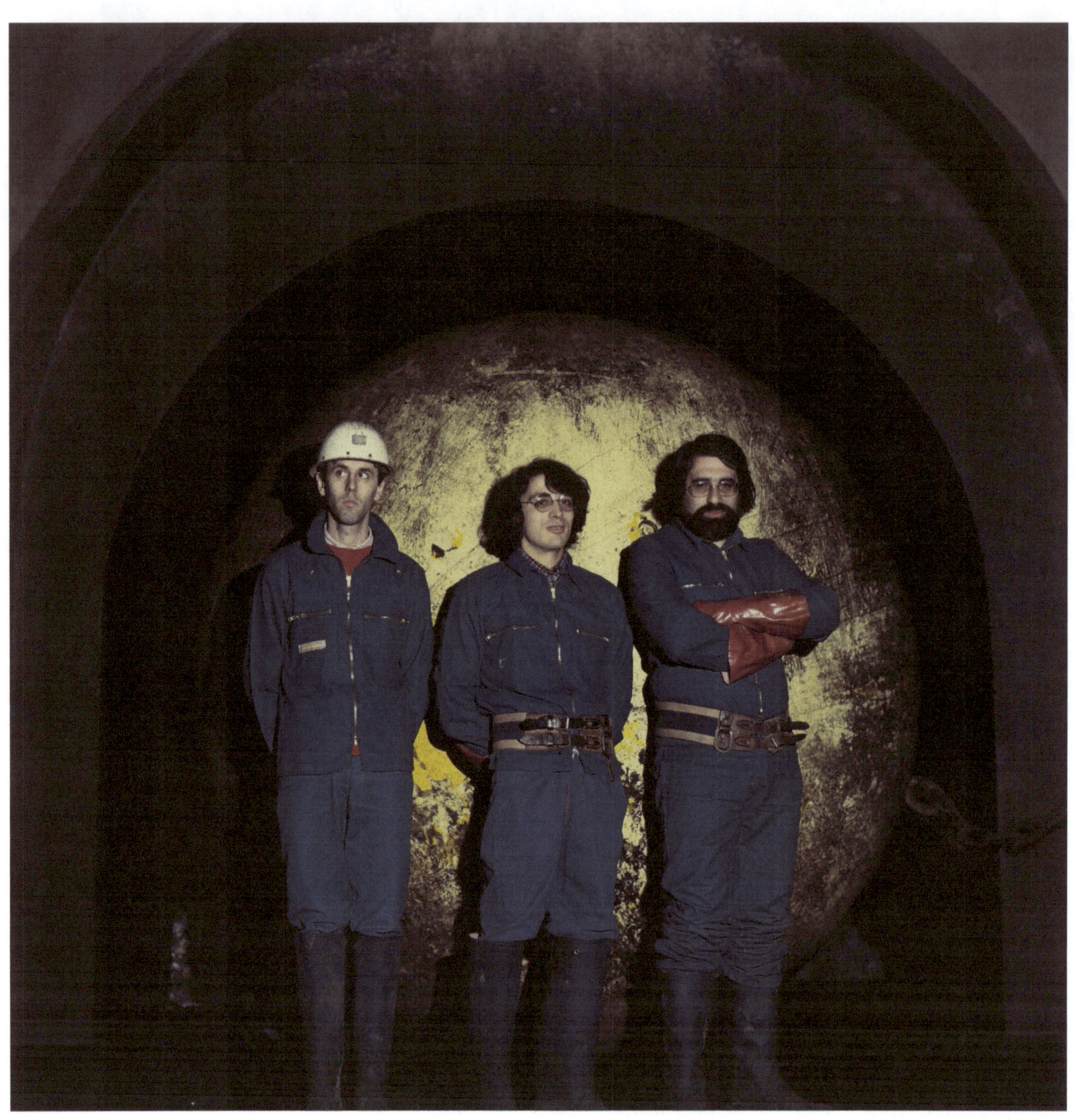

Sewers workers

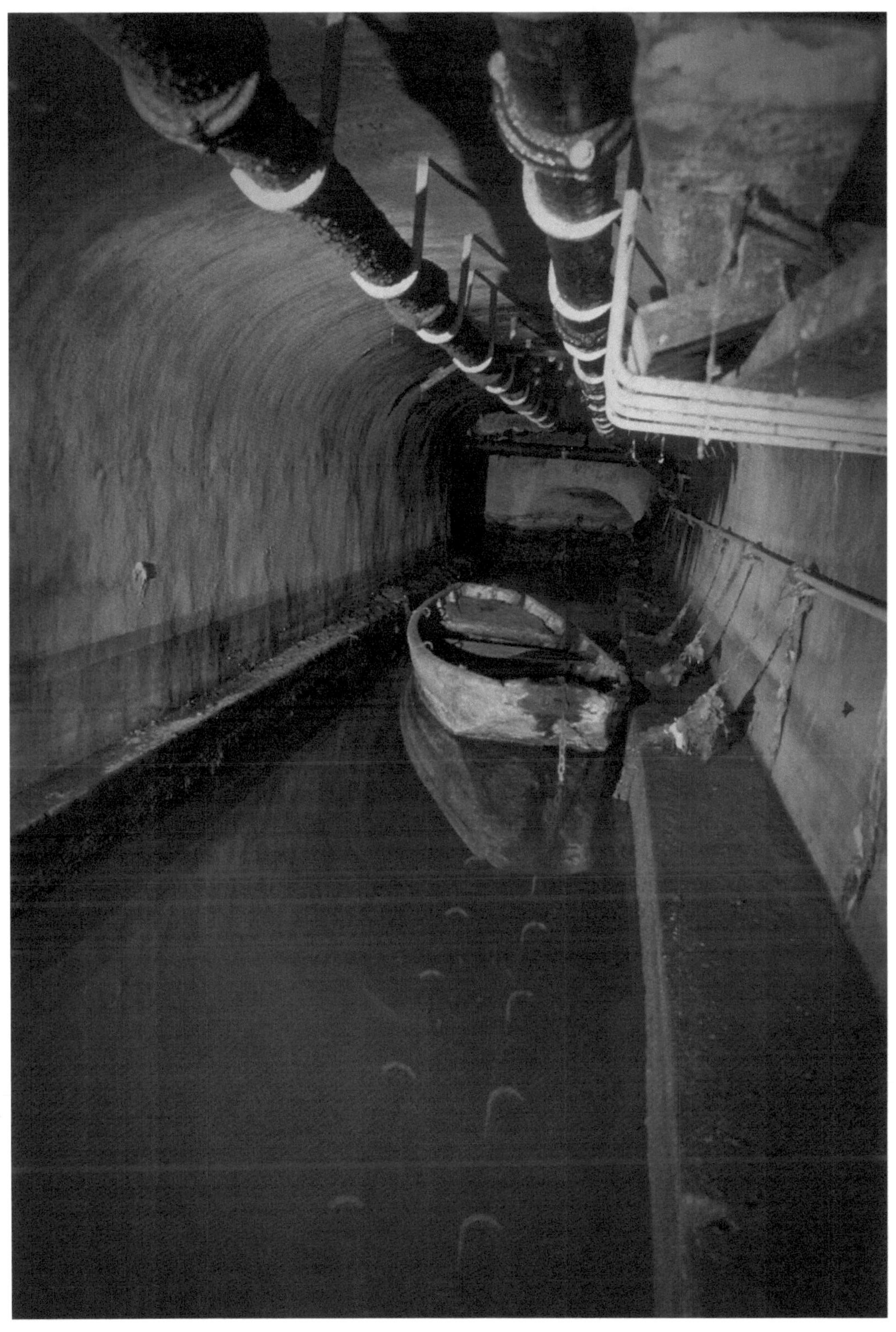

The sewers are a complex river networks where workers travel in small boats.

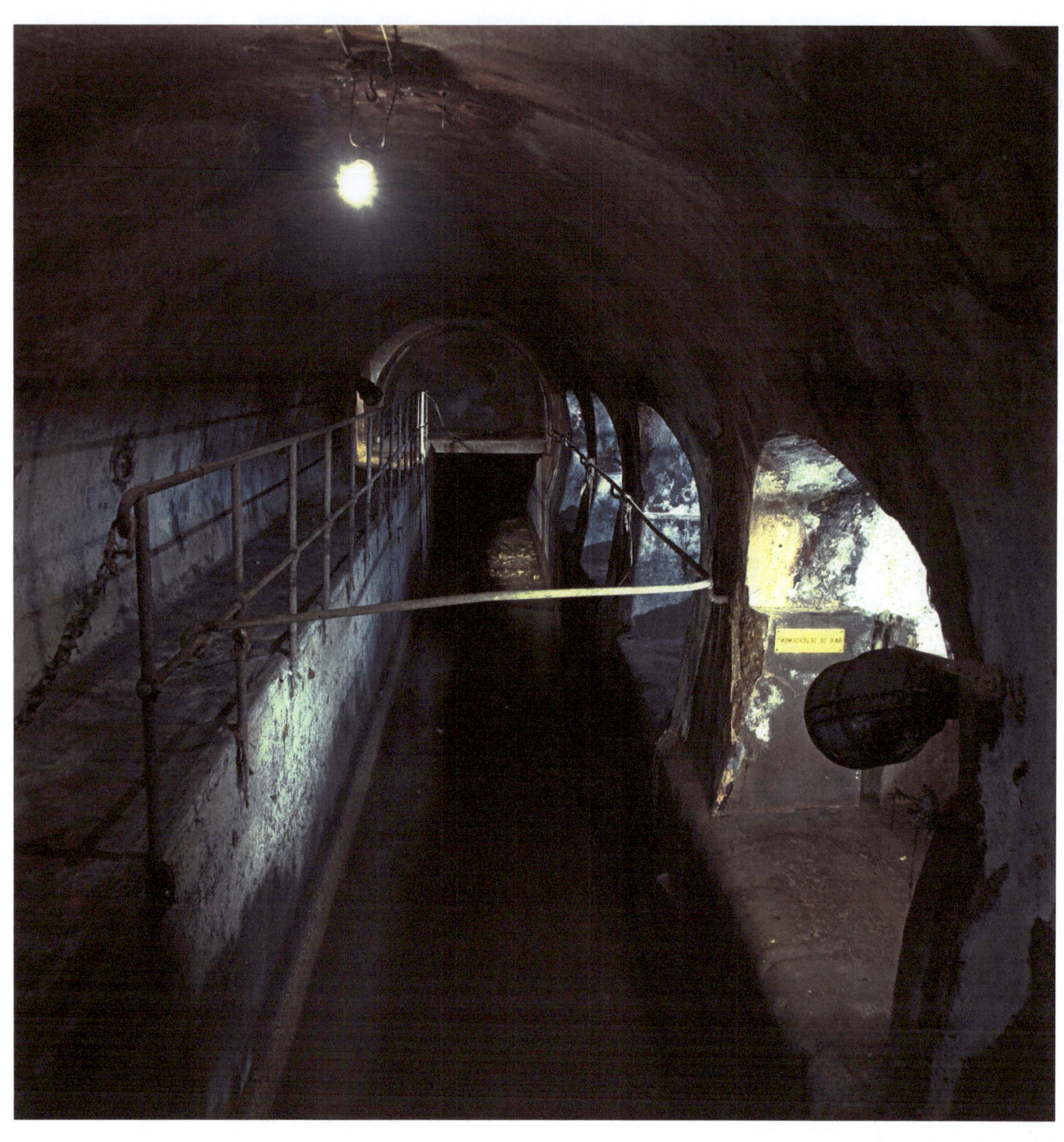

Each street at the surface corresponds a sewer. The surface of Paris has its exact duplicate of sewer network.

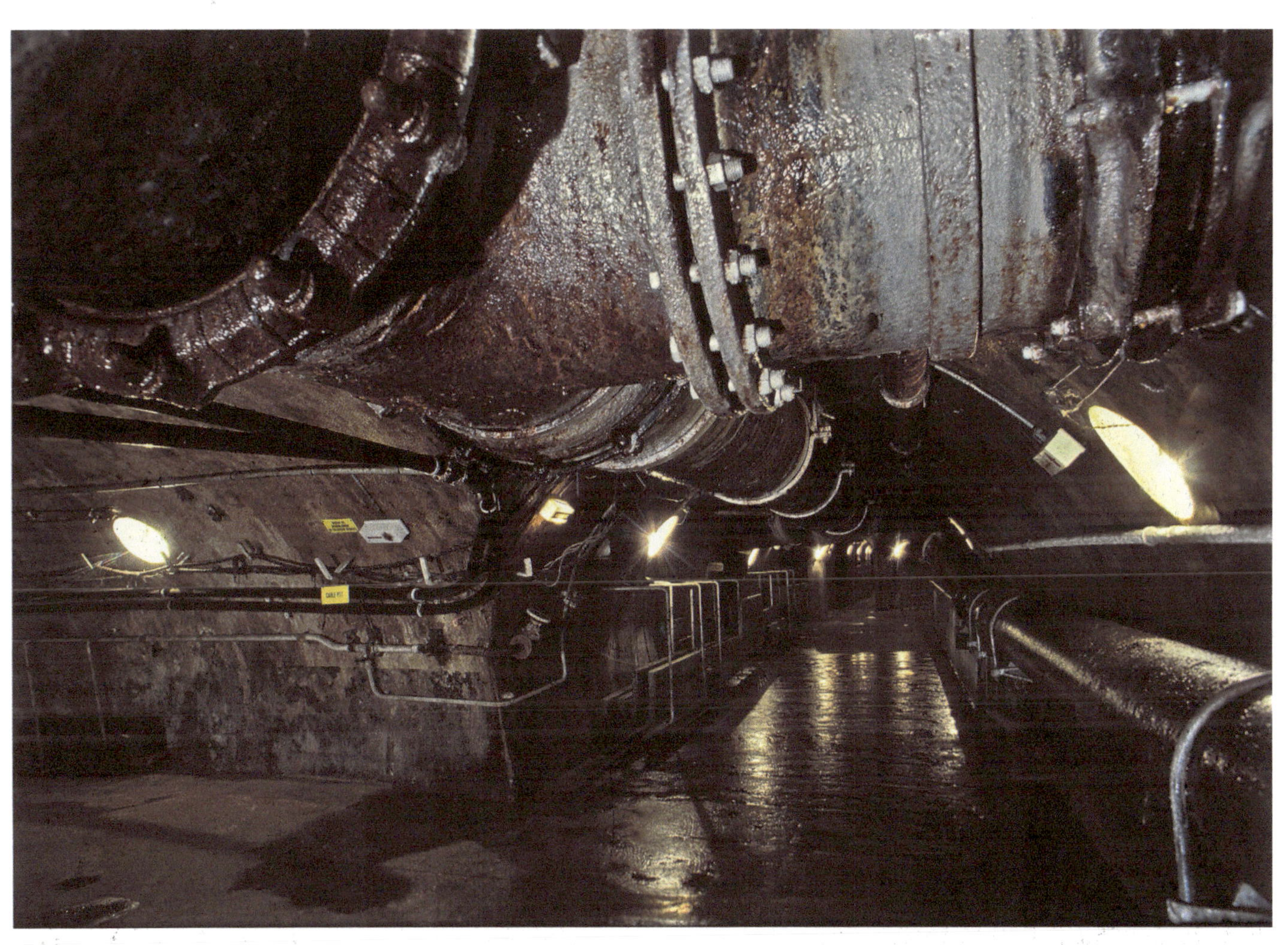

Telecomunication, drinkable water and pneumatic network (a system used until 1984 by the postal service to send letters in special pipes with compressed air for immediate delivery) run through the sewer.

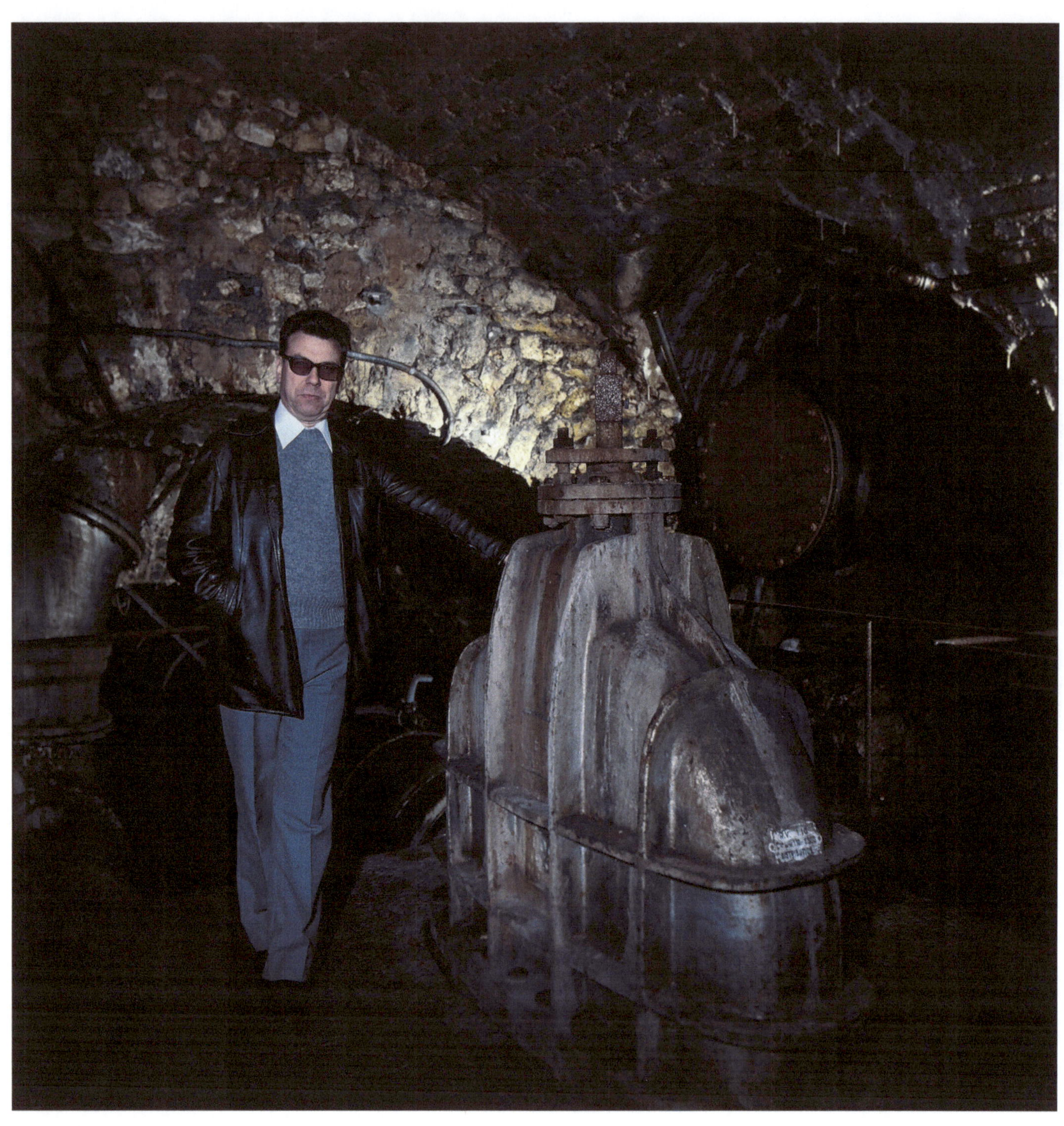

Man in charge of the sewers

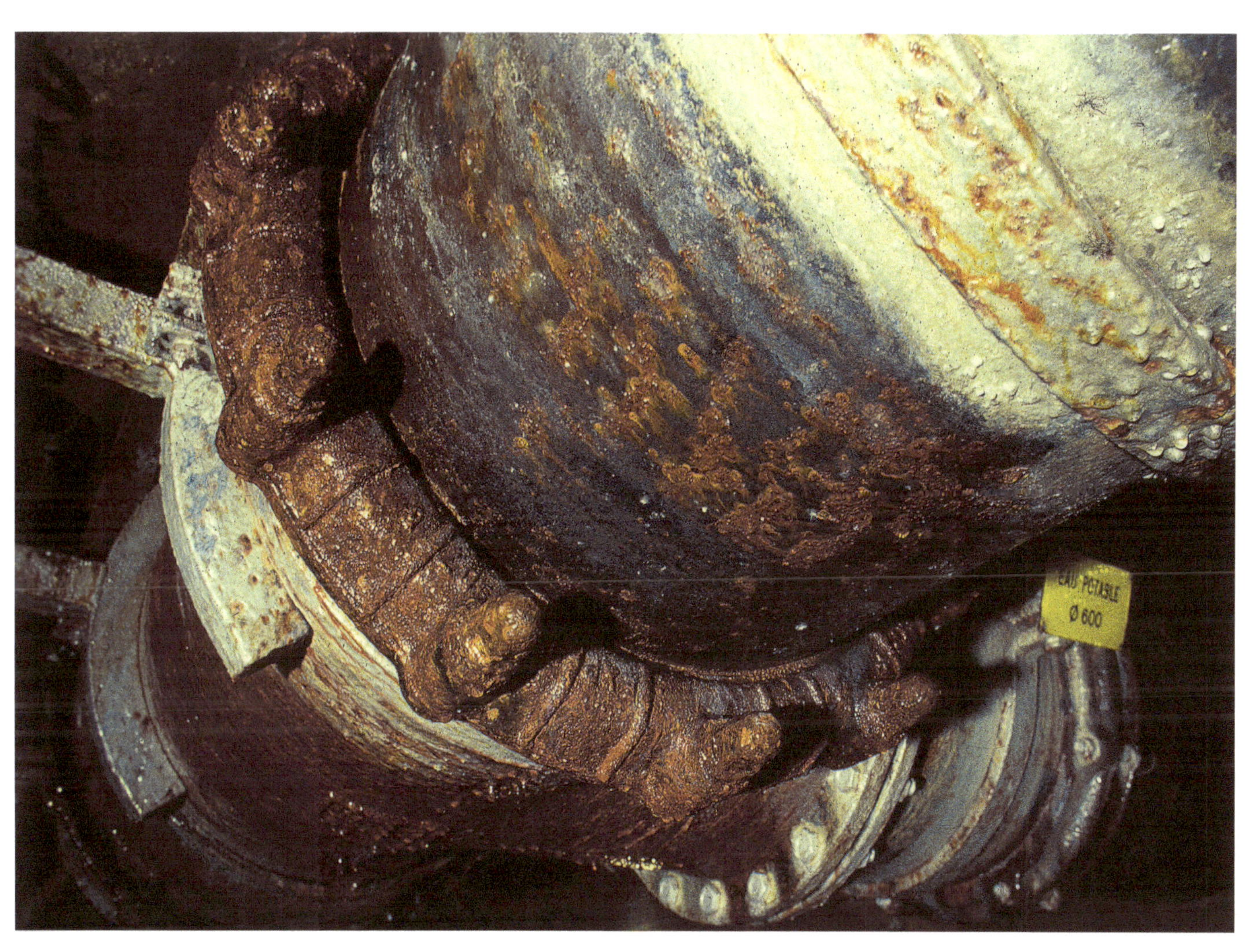

Drinkable water pipe. Clean and waste water run together under the city

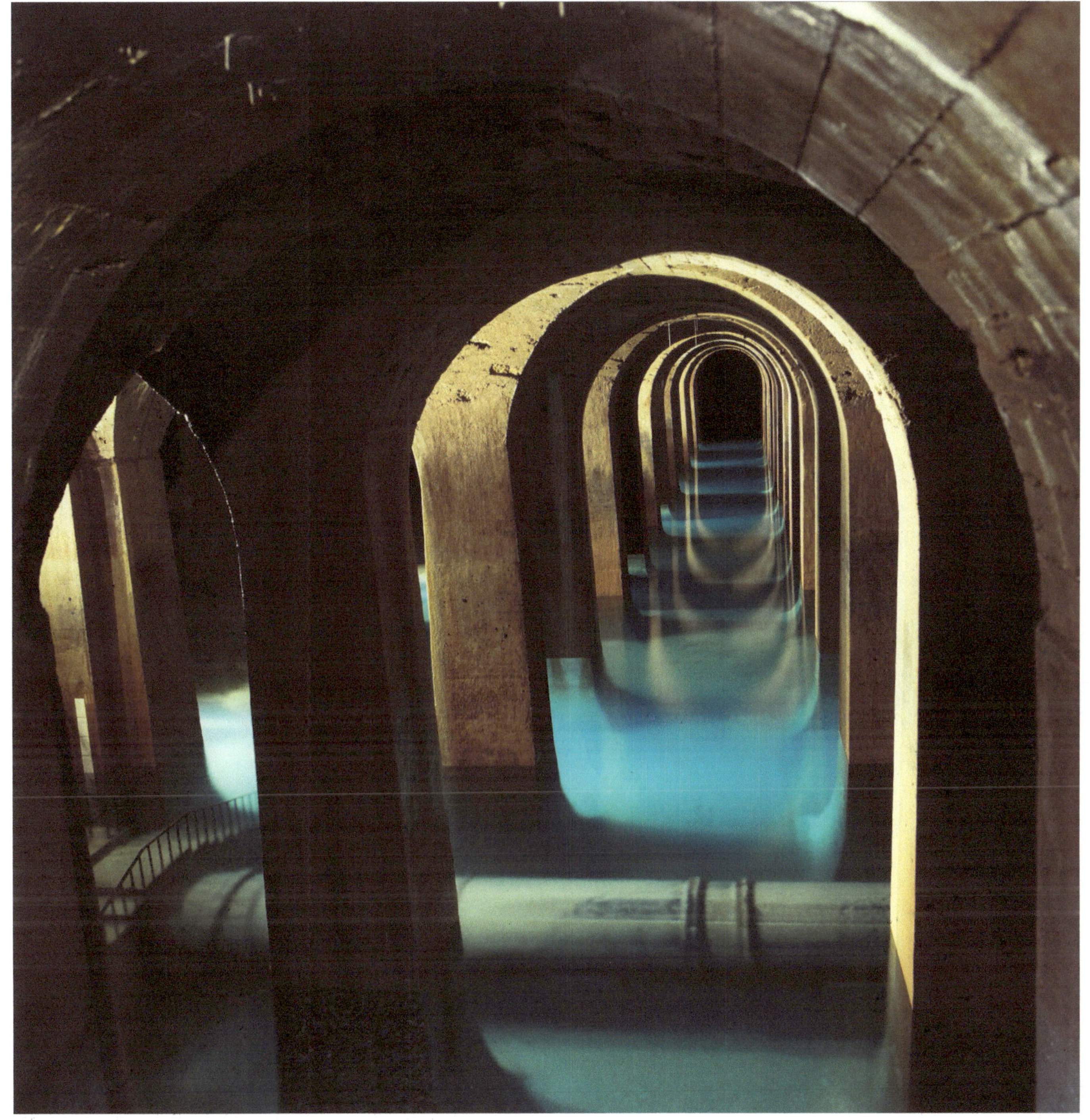

CHAPTER FIVE: THE MONTSOURIS WATER RESERVOIR

The reservoir is composed of 2 underground levels, which contain a total of 53,521,257 gallons of water. The most amazing fact is that it sits on nothing! Only quarries. A total of 1,800 pillars were needed to support such a weight. The work was finished in 1872.

Lower reservoir

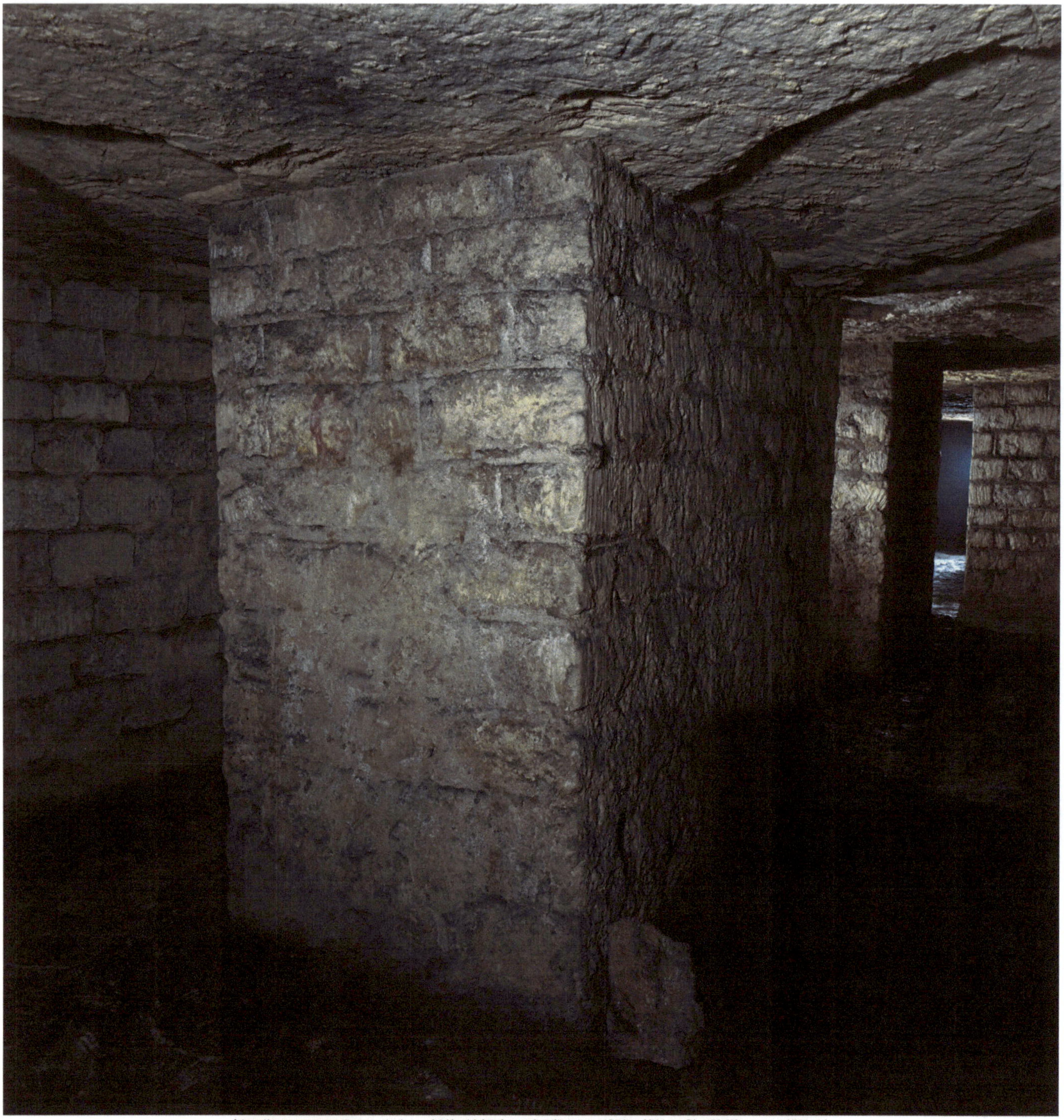

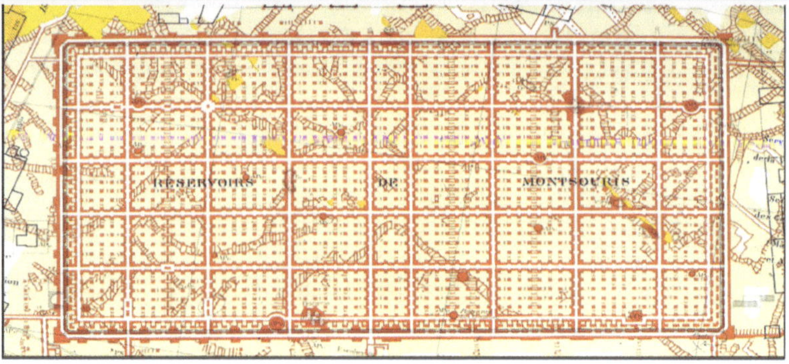
RESERVOIRS DE MONTSOURIS

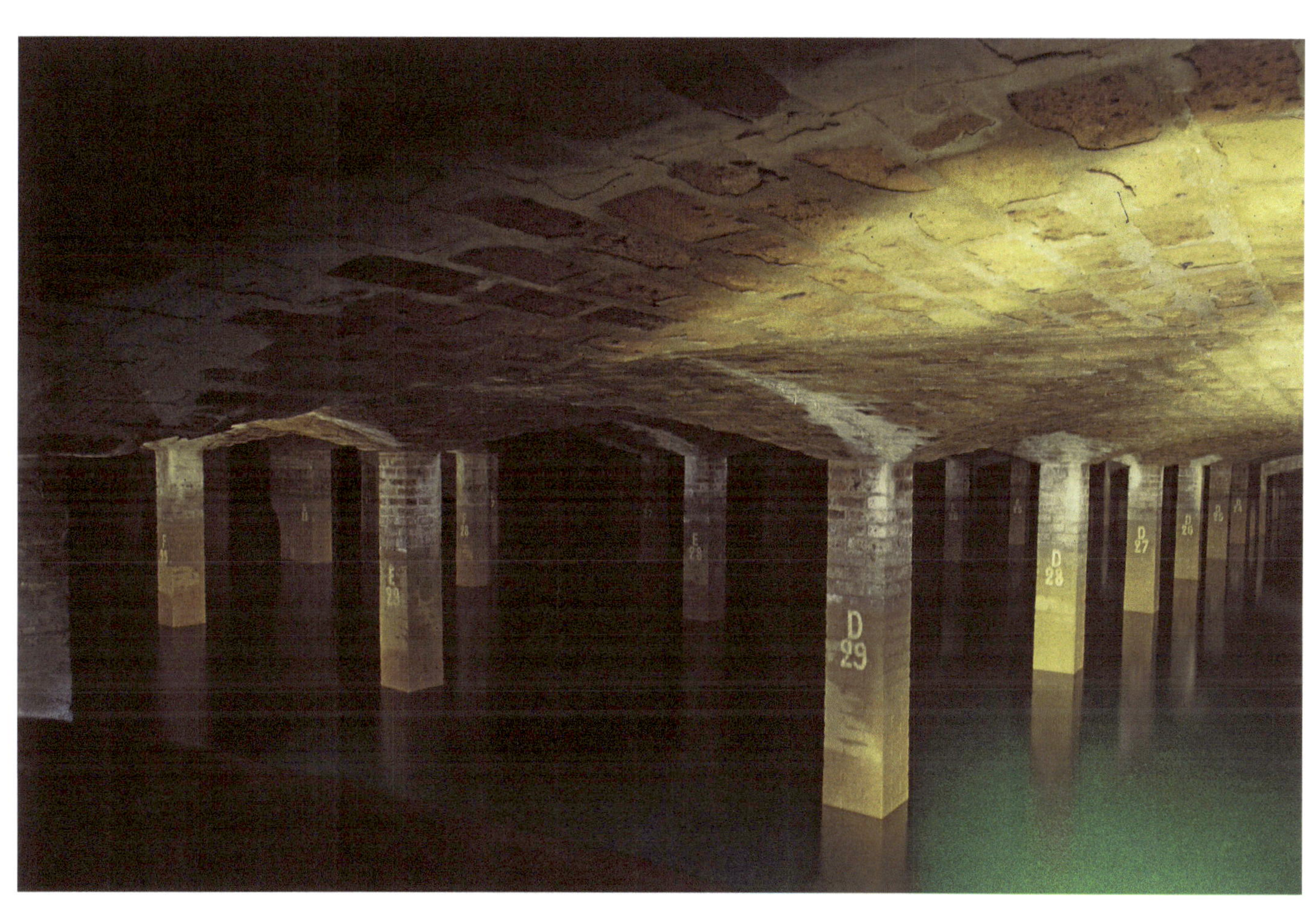

above image: upper reservoir

left images: supporting pillar and quarry map of the reservoir

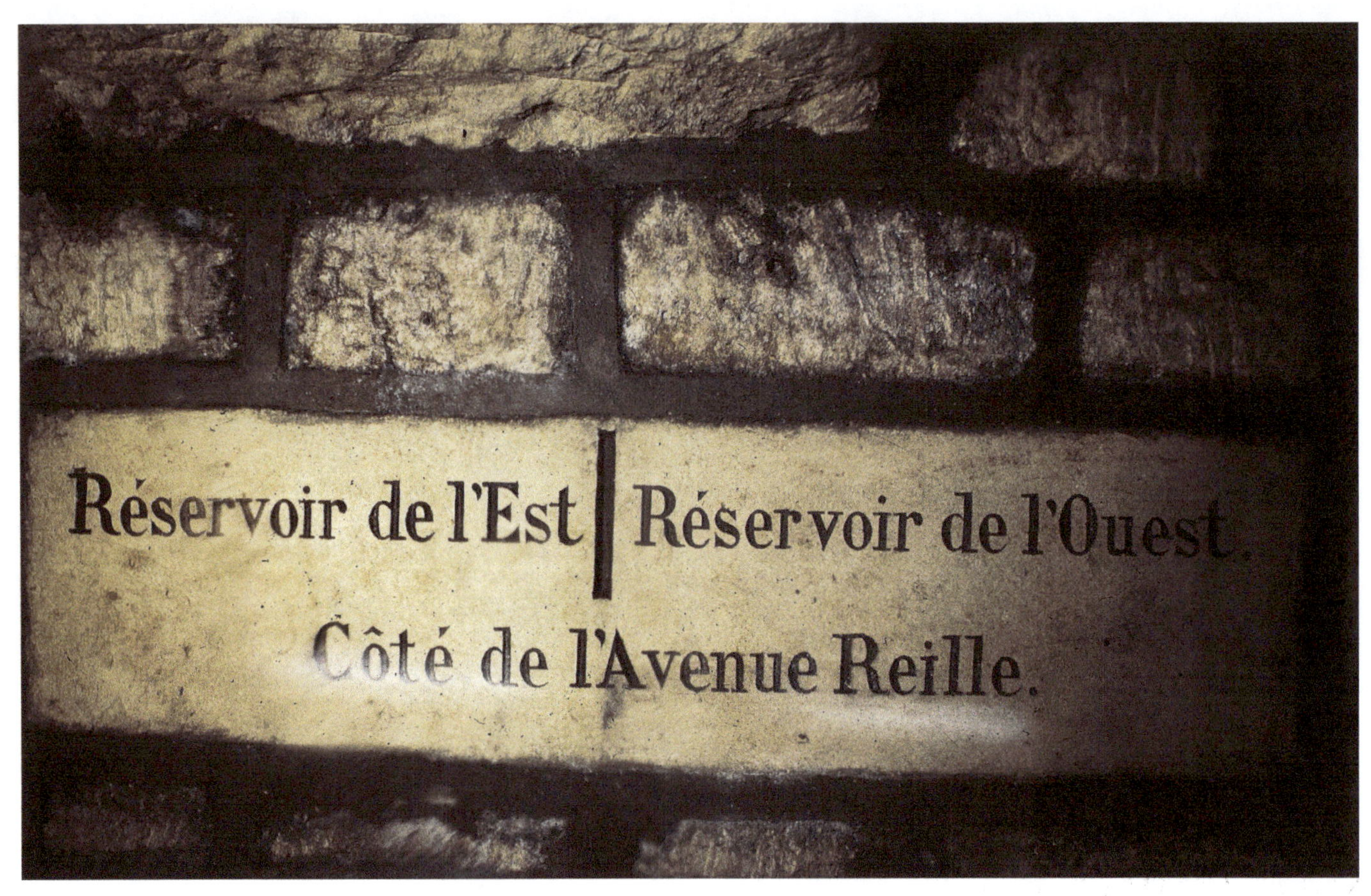

Stone carved sign in the quarries. East / West reservoir on Reille avenue side

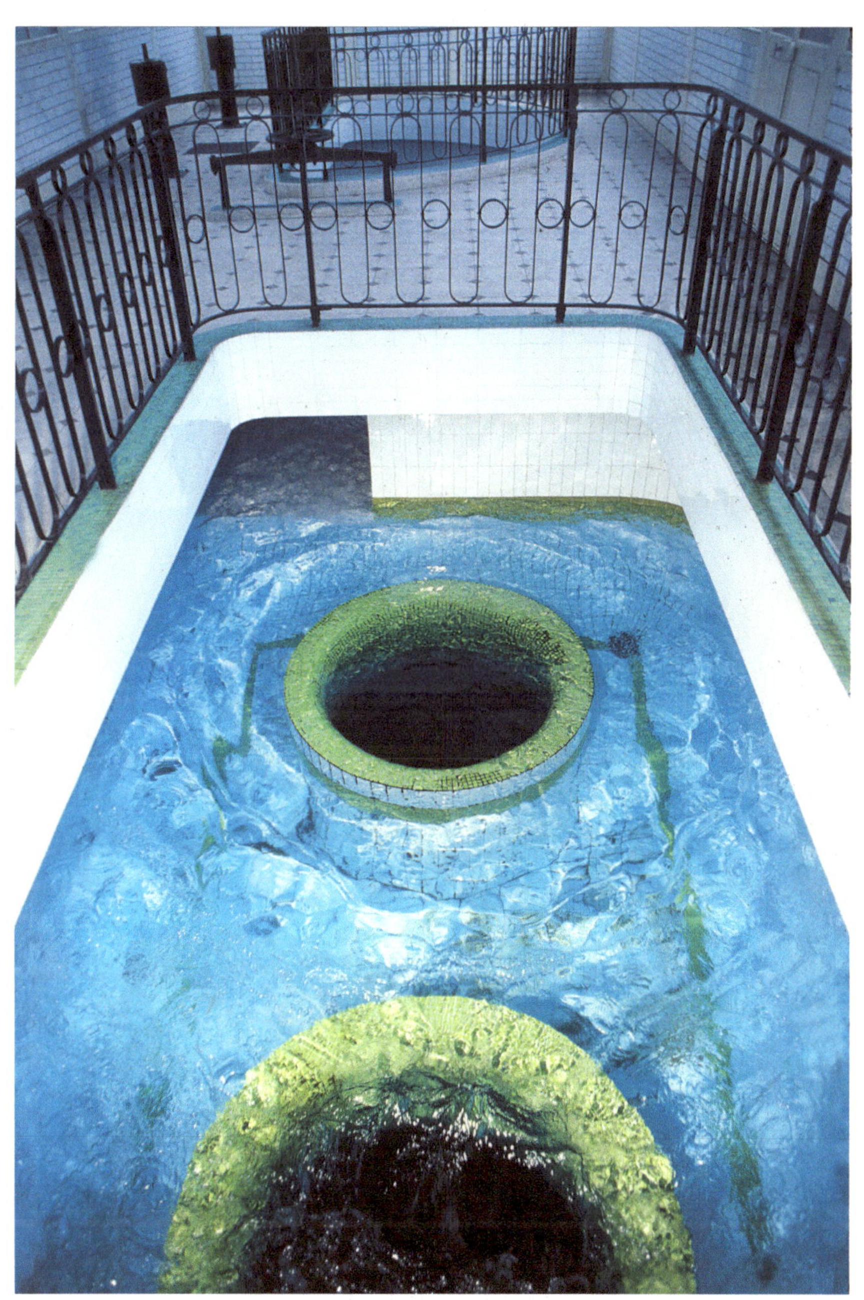

Point of arrival of spring water. Before pouring into the reservoir a small water sample passes throught a fish tank where lives a carp. As long as the fish looks healthy, the water is “assumed” clean.

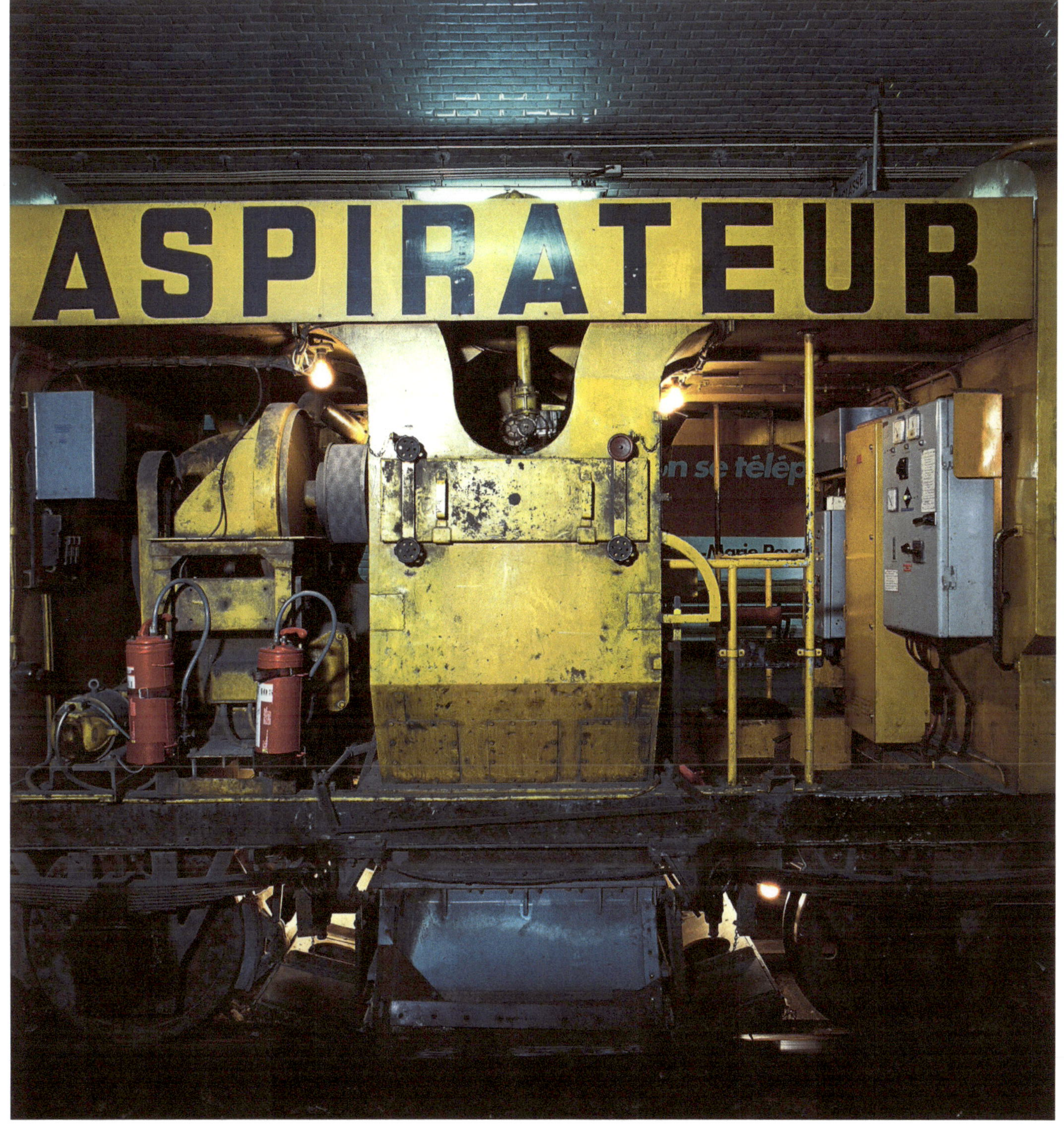

CHAPTER SIX: THE SUBWAY

“The Metropolitain” was open in 1900. It is a strange mix of century old engineering and cutting edge technology. Most likely most of the machinery photographed in this book doesn’t exist anymore …

From 1 to 5 am, when the subway closes, the vacuum cleaner cart (Aspitateur) sucks all trash from the railways

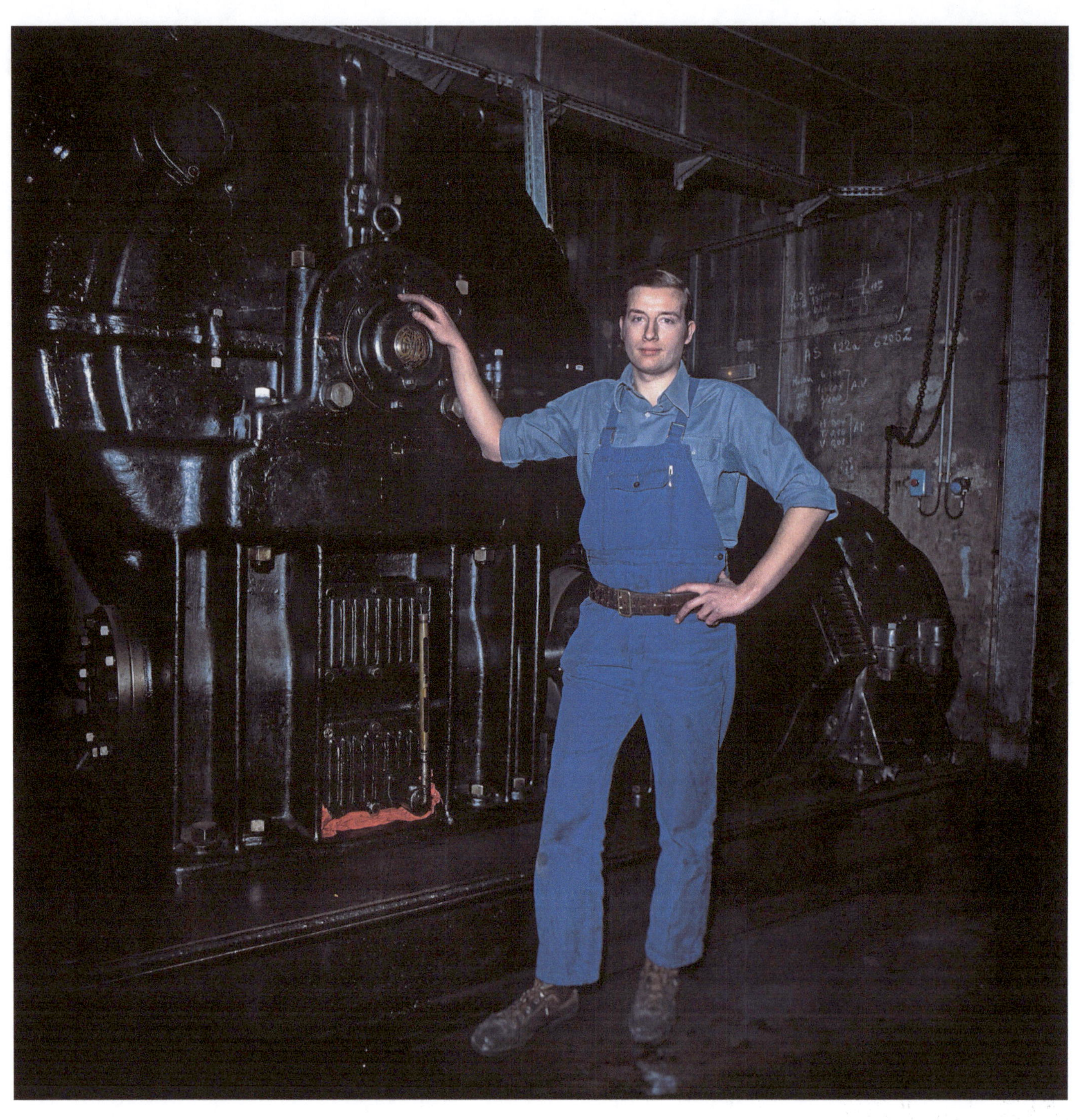

Maintenance worker posig next to the gigantic escalator motor of the station "Place des Fetes" the oldest of Paris

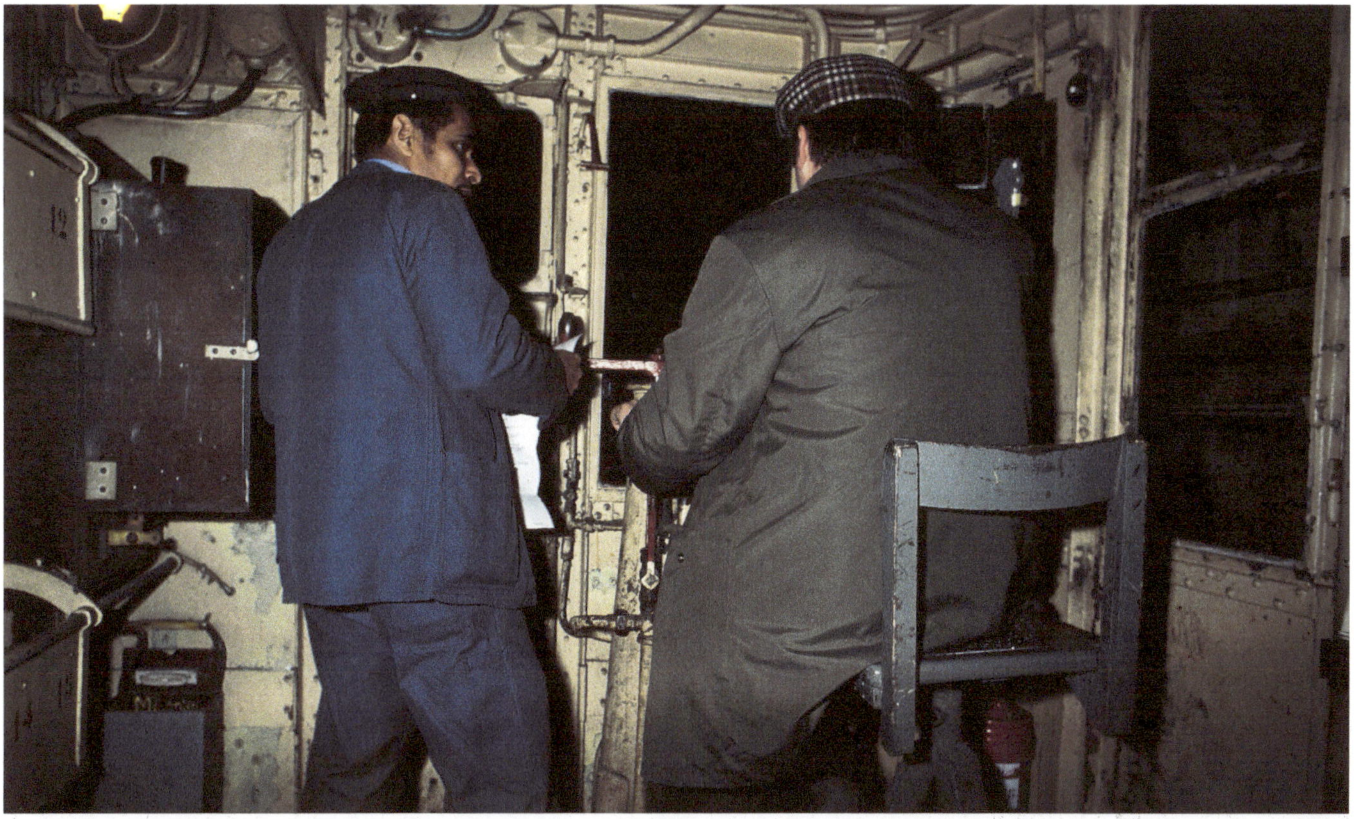

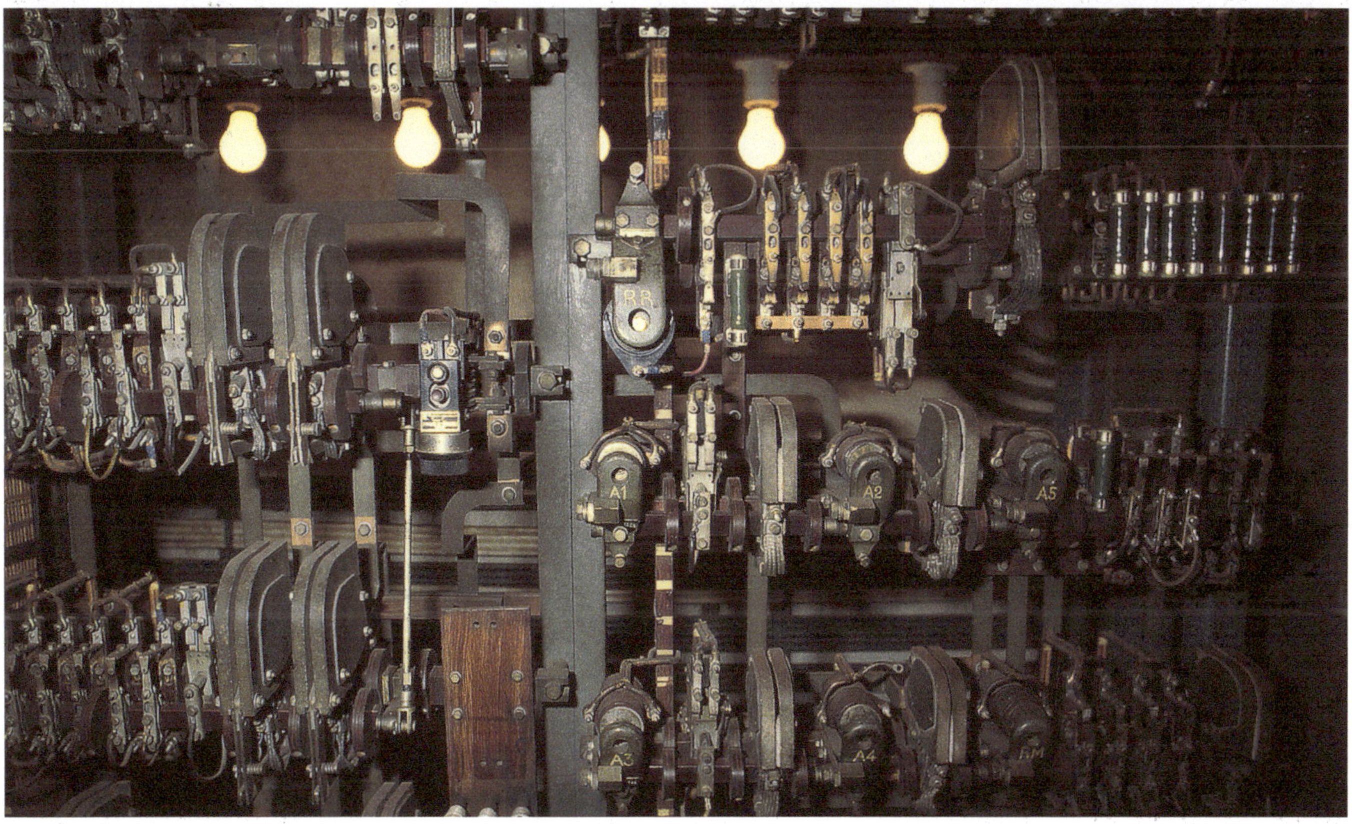

top image: train pilot and co-pilot in cockpit
bottom image: station fuse box

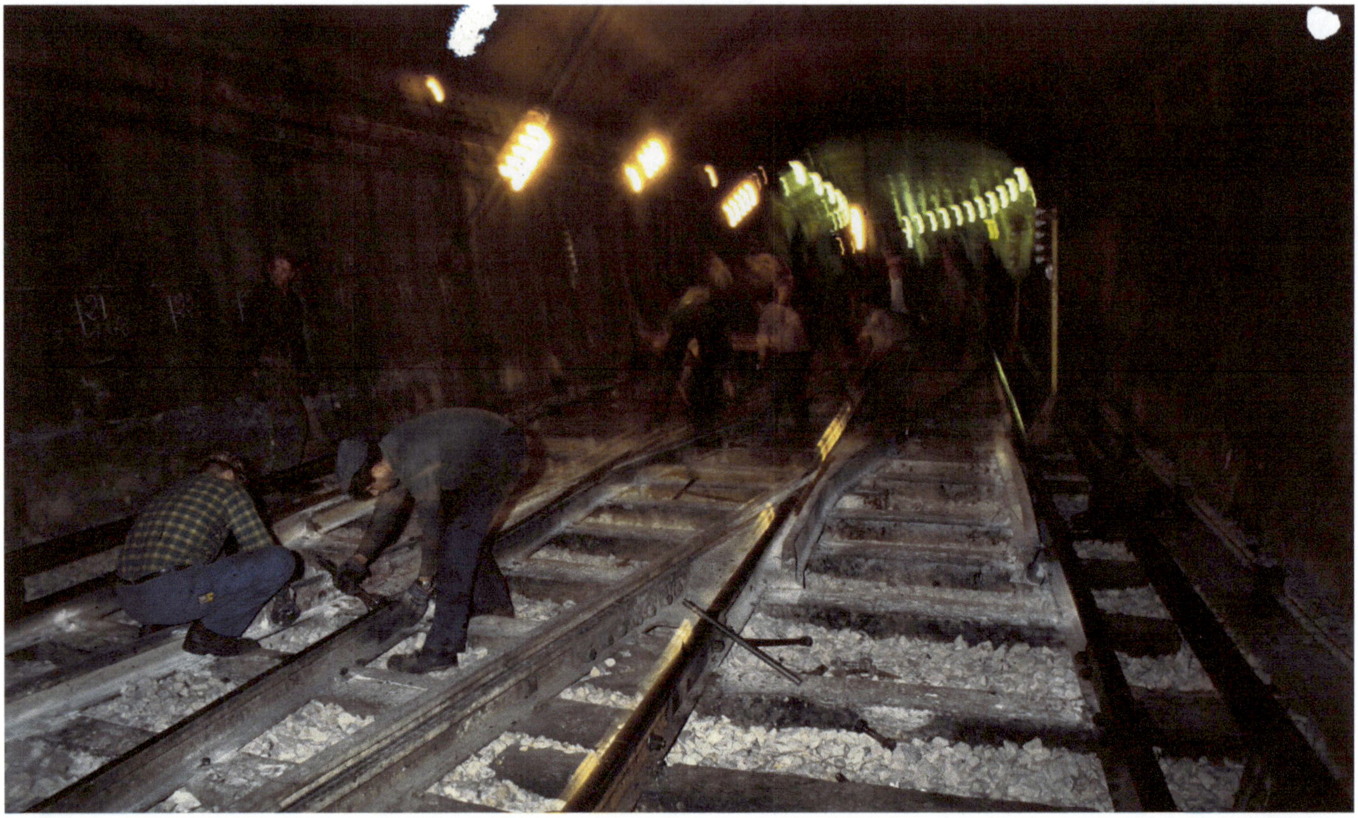

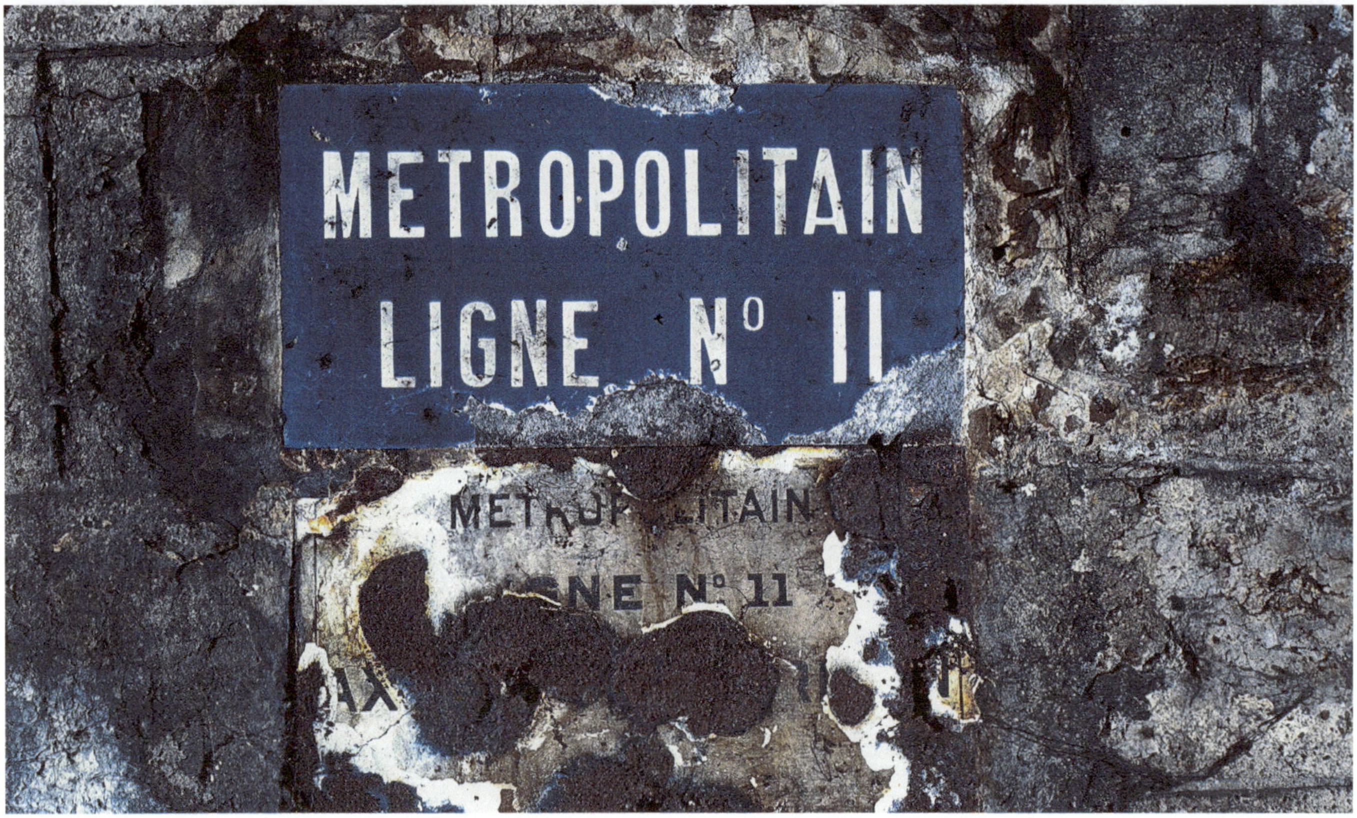

top image: night repairs from 1 to 5 am, while the subway is closed
bottom image: signs in the quarries under the subway

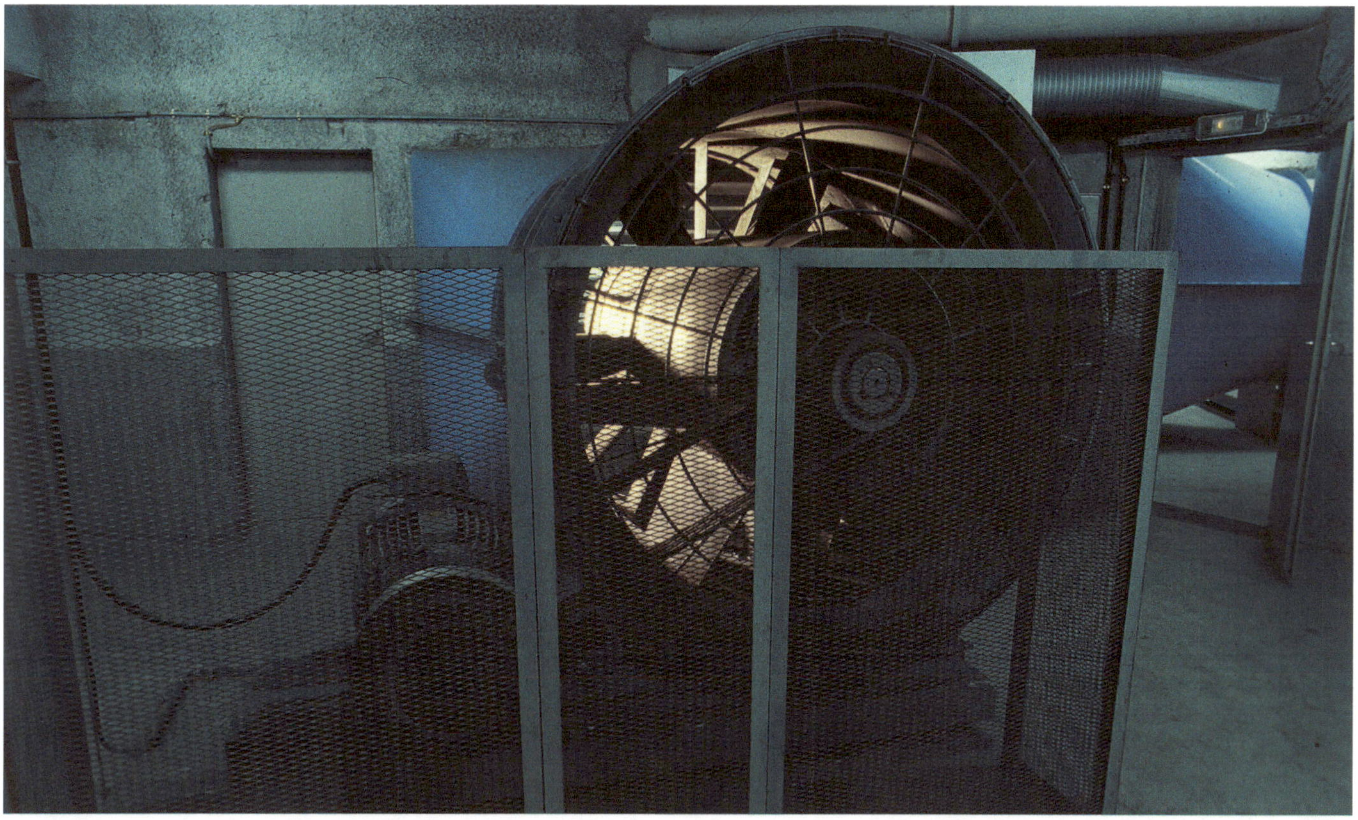

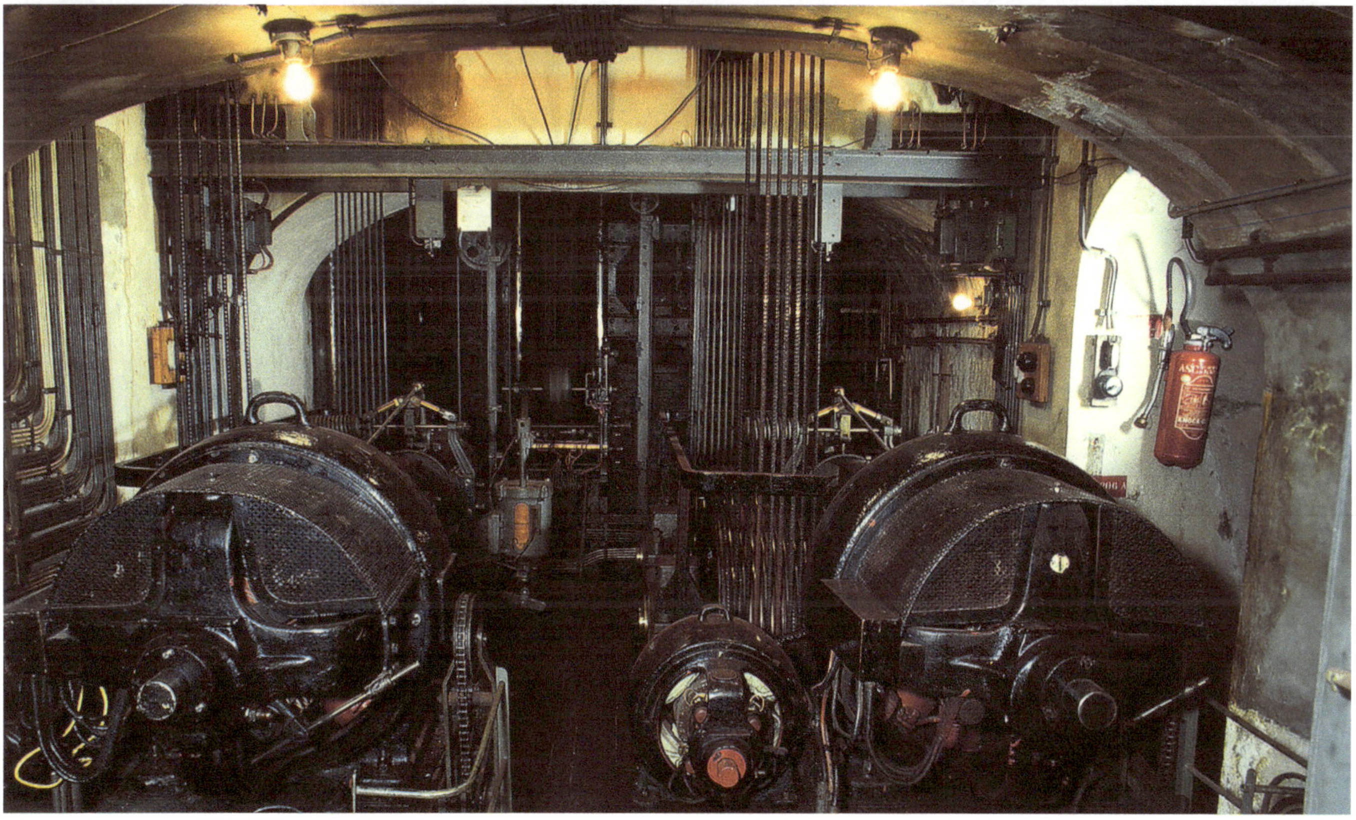

top image: fire emergency fan
bottom image: elevators motors

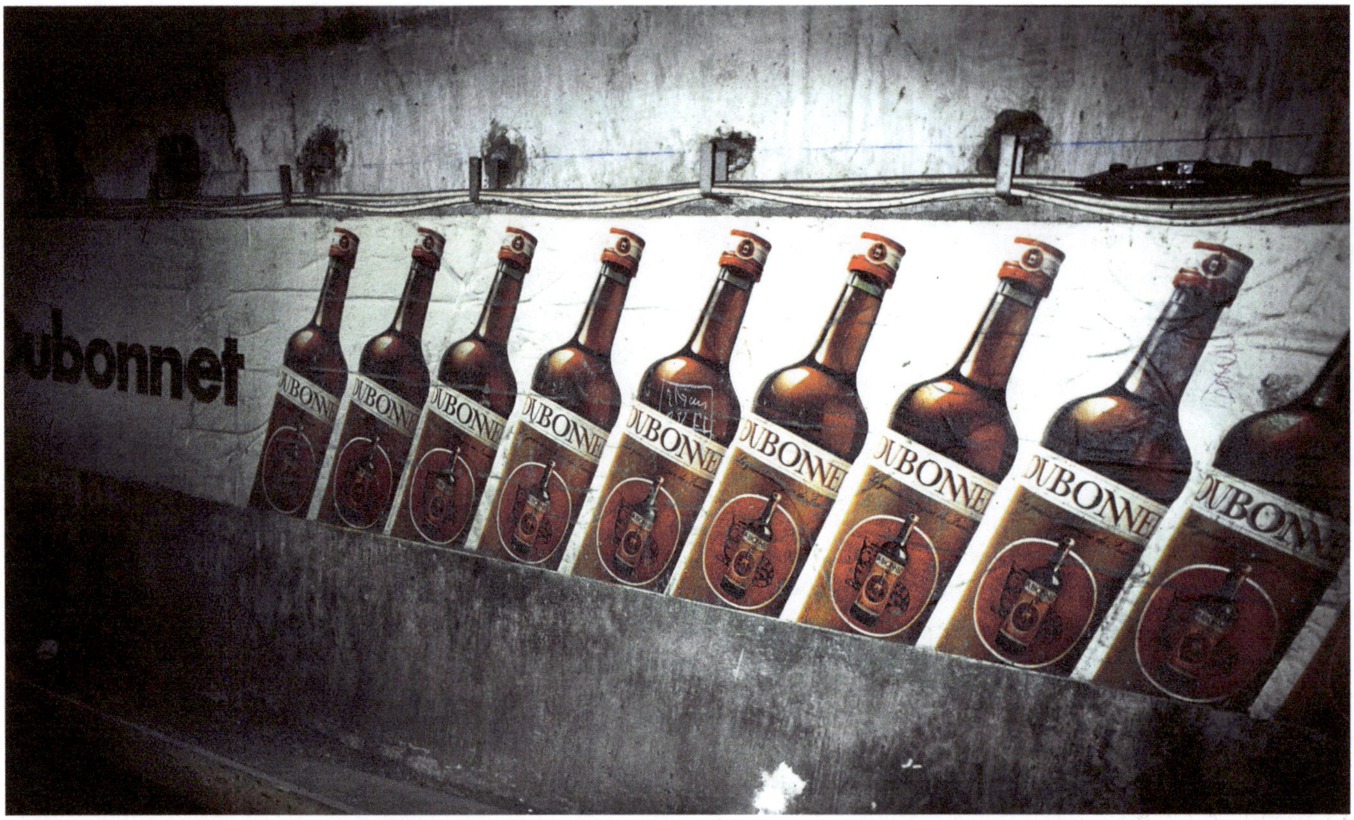

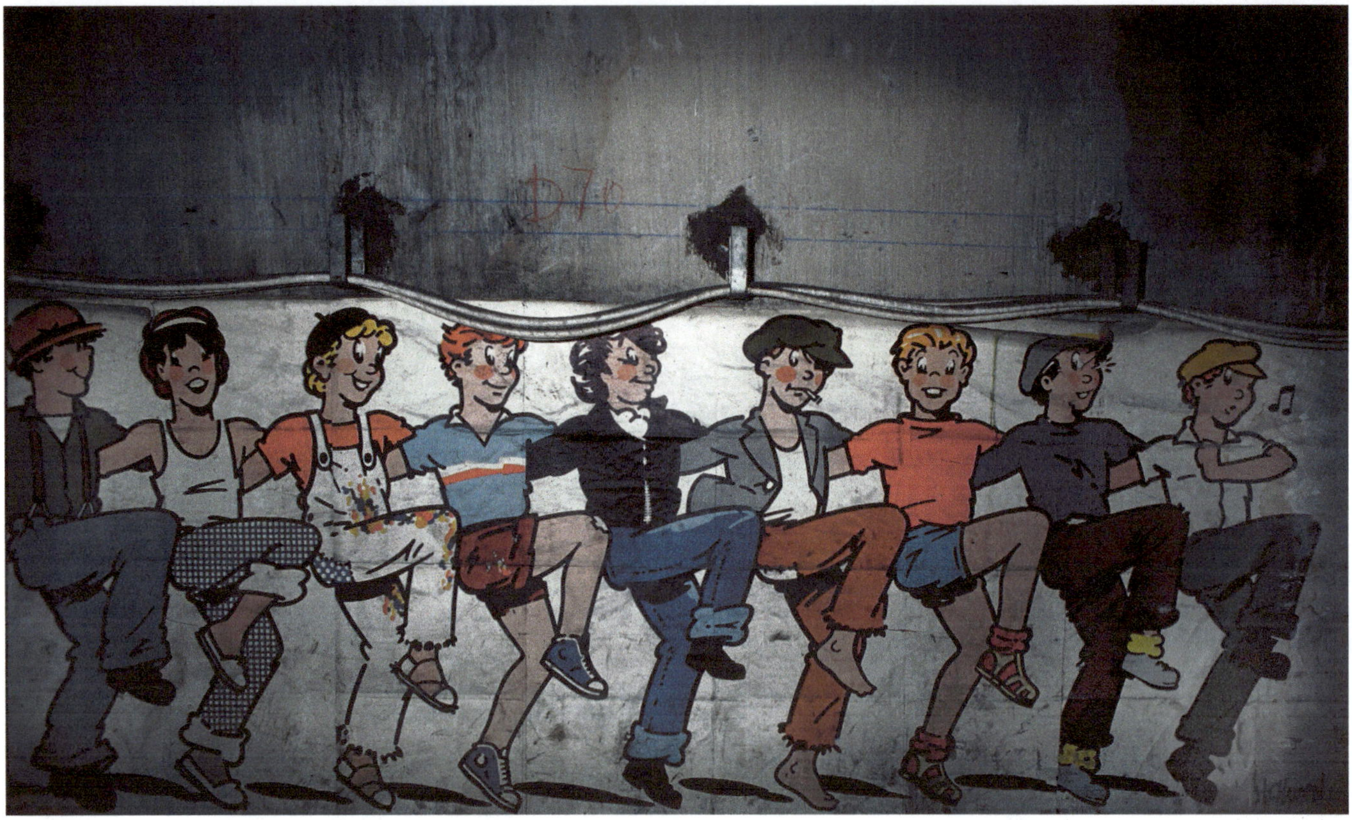

Vintage 1950's advertising for a popular alcoholic drink. To be read while train running

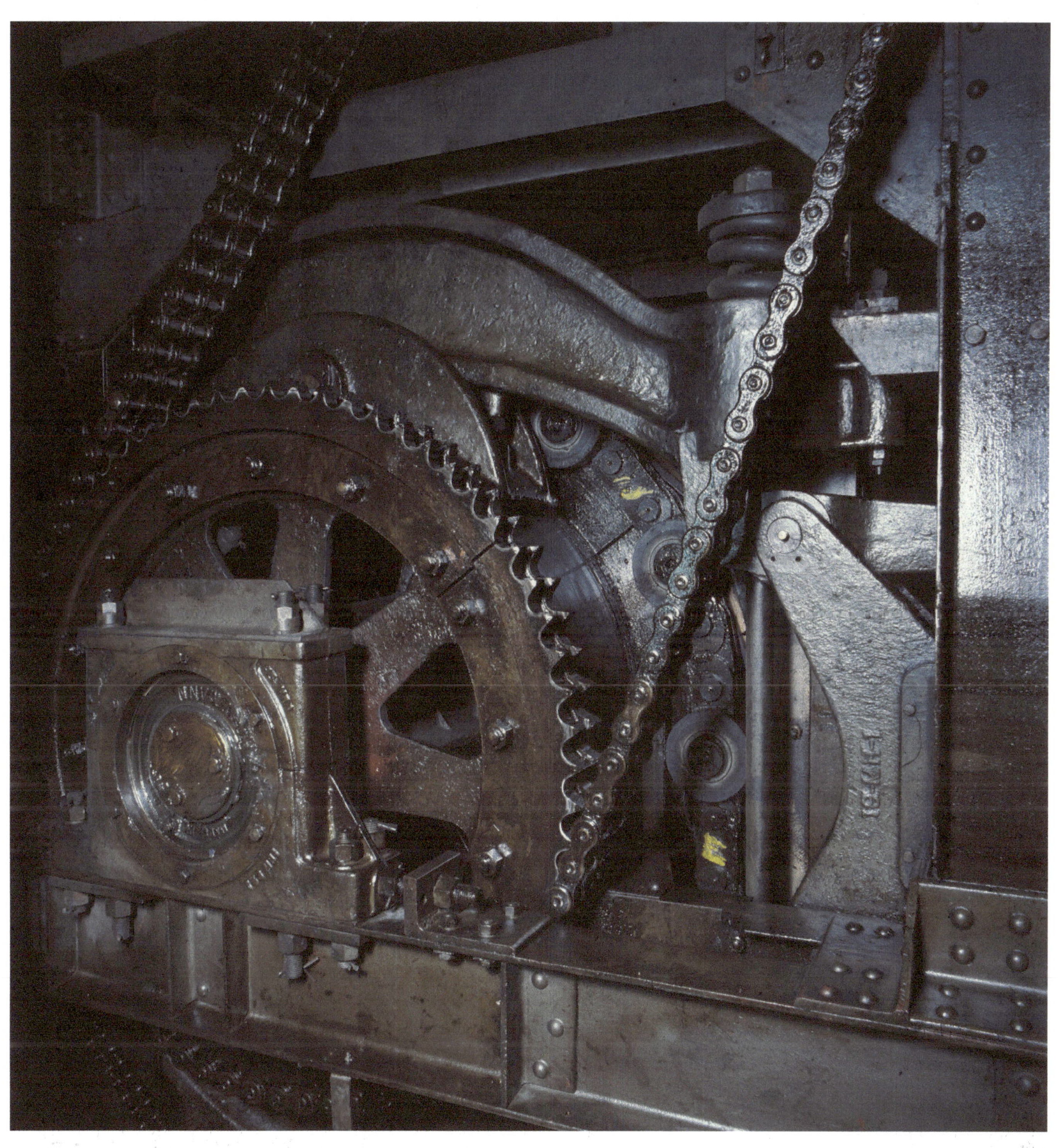

Giant 7 feet toothed escalator wheel at the sation "Place des Fetes".

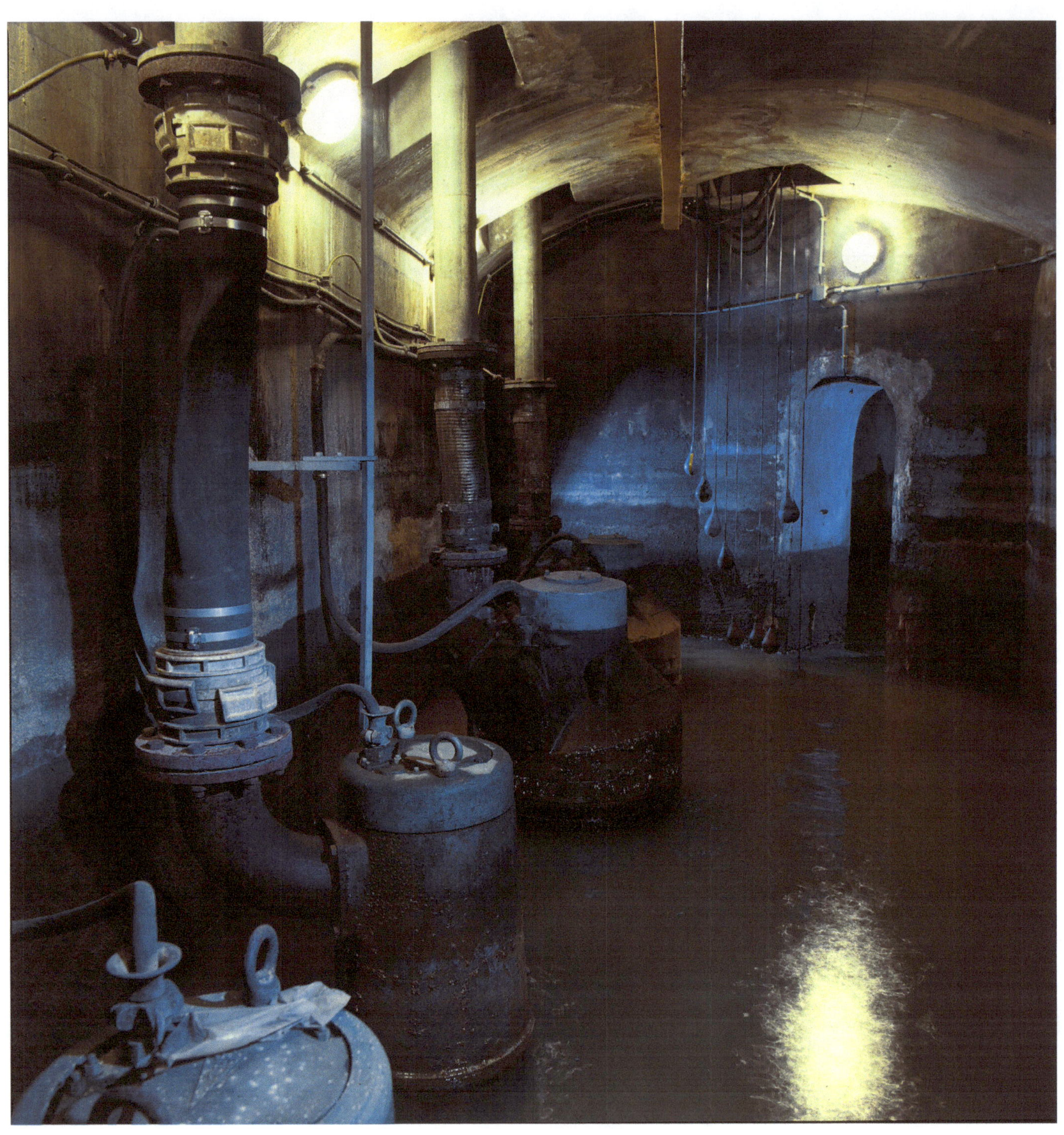

Water pumping chamber under the Seine River

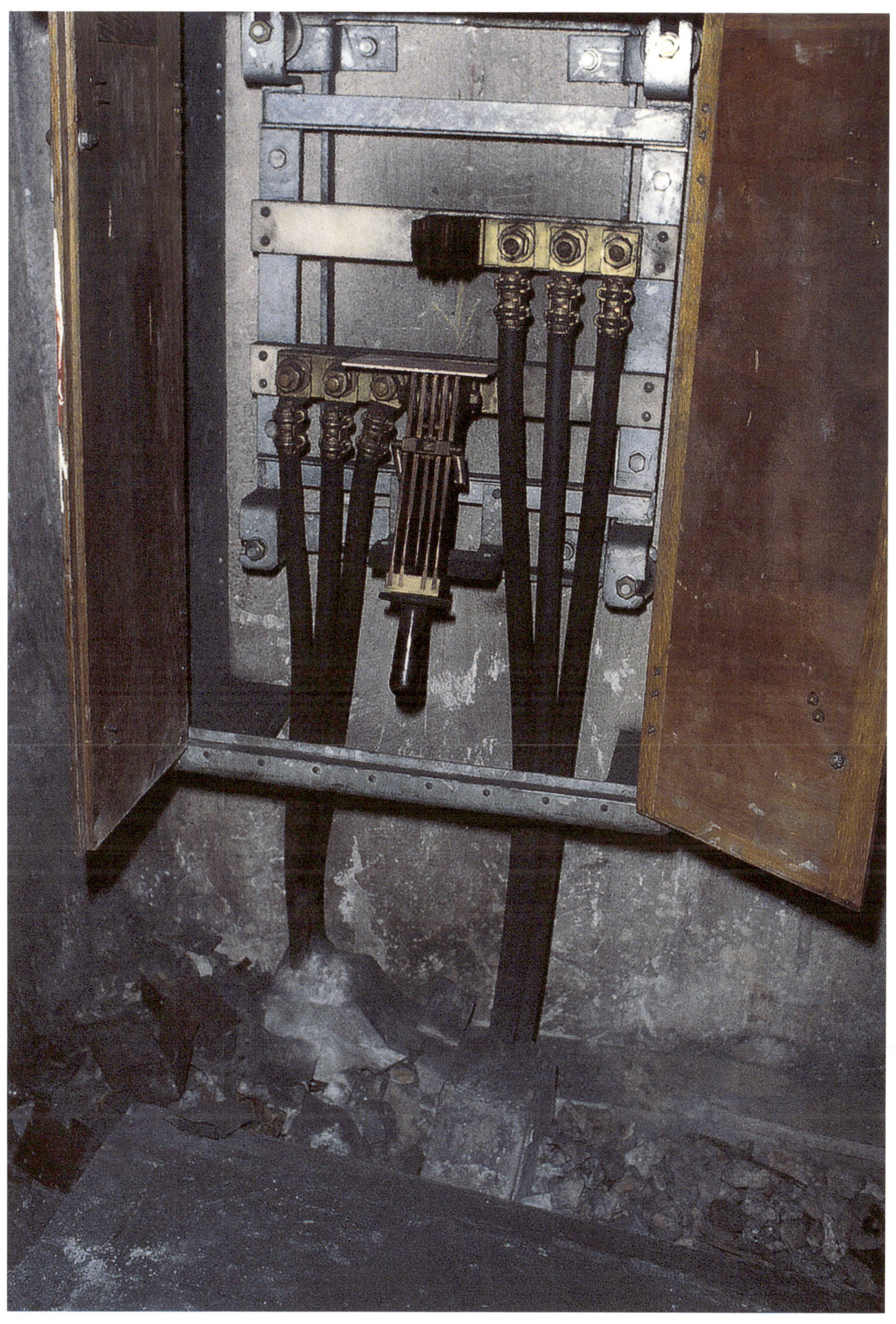

Security switch on "off" position while the workers repair the hight voltage electric rails.

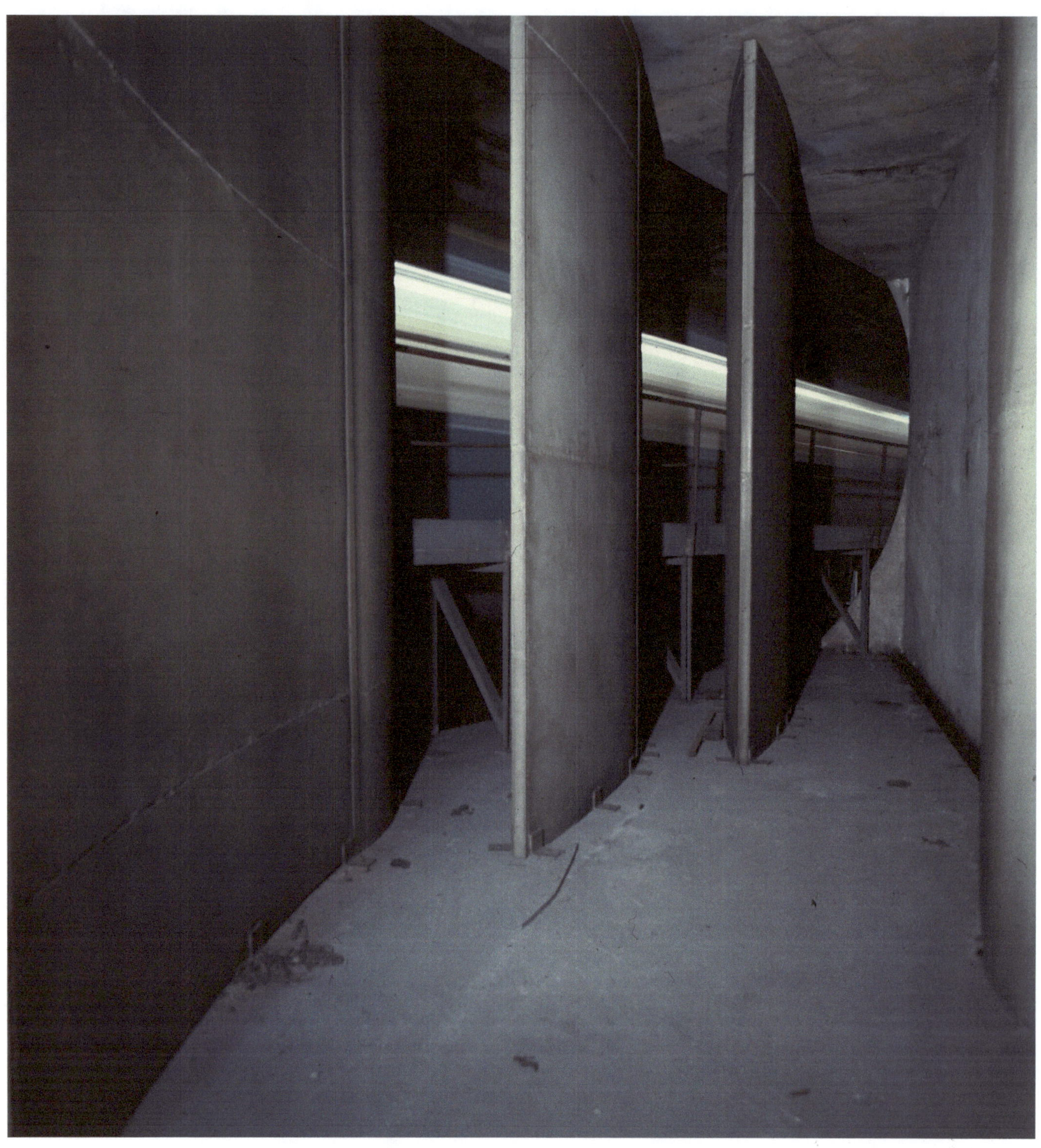

Decompression shaft in the RER line (fast train) to prevent the "piston effect" that would push a mass of air into the station and blow passengers away. The "fins" divert the air pressure into the main shaft which ends at street level covered by a metal grid in the sidewalk. Since people walk on the grid, the air blown is calculated to be too weak to lift a woman 's skirt ...

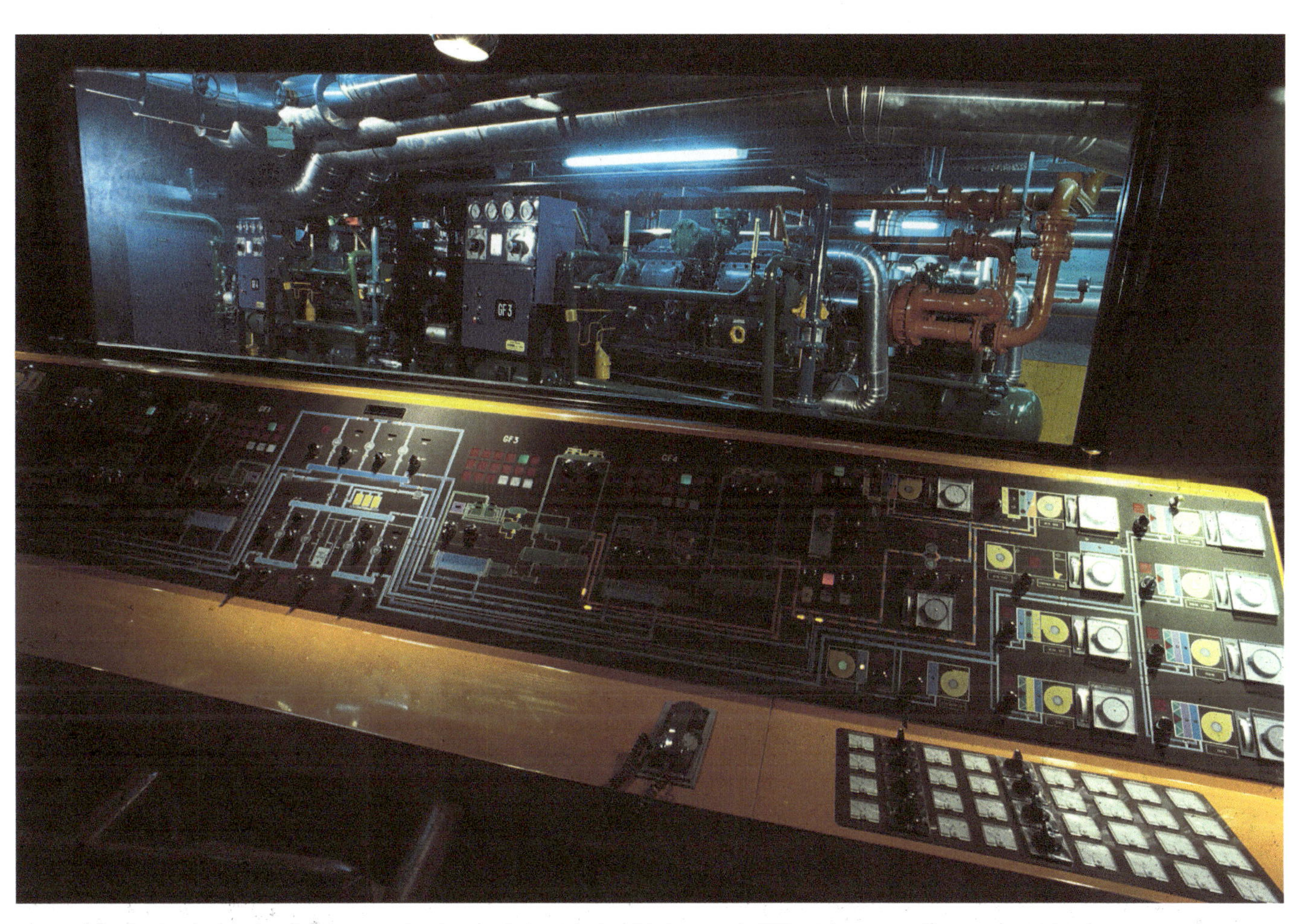

RER control center at Gare de Lyon station. The station is built in ground water, and actually floats. A system of pumps keeps the train station levelled, and the rails tracks aligned

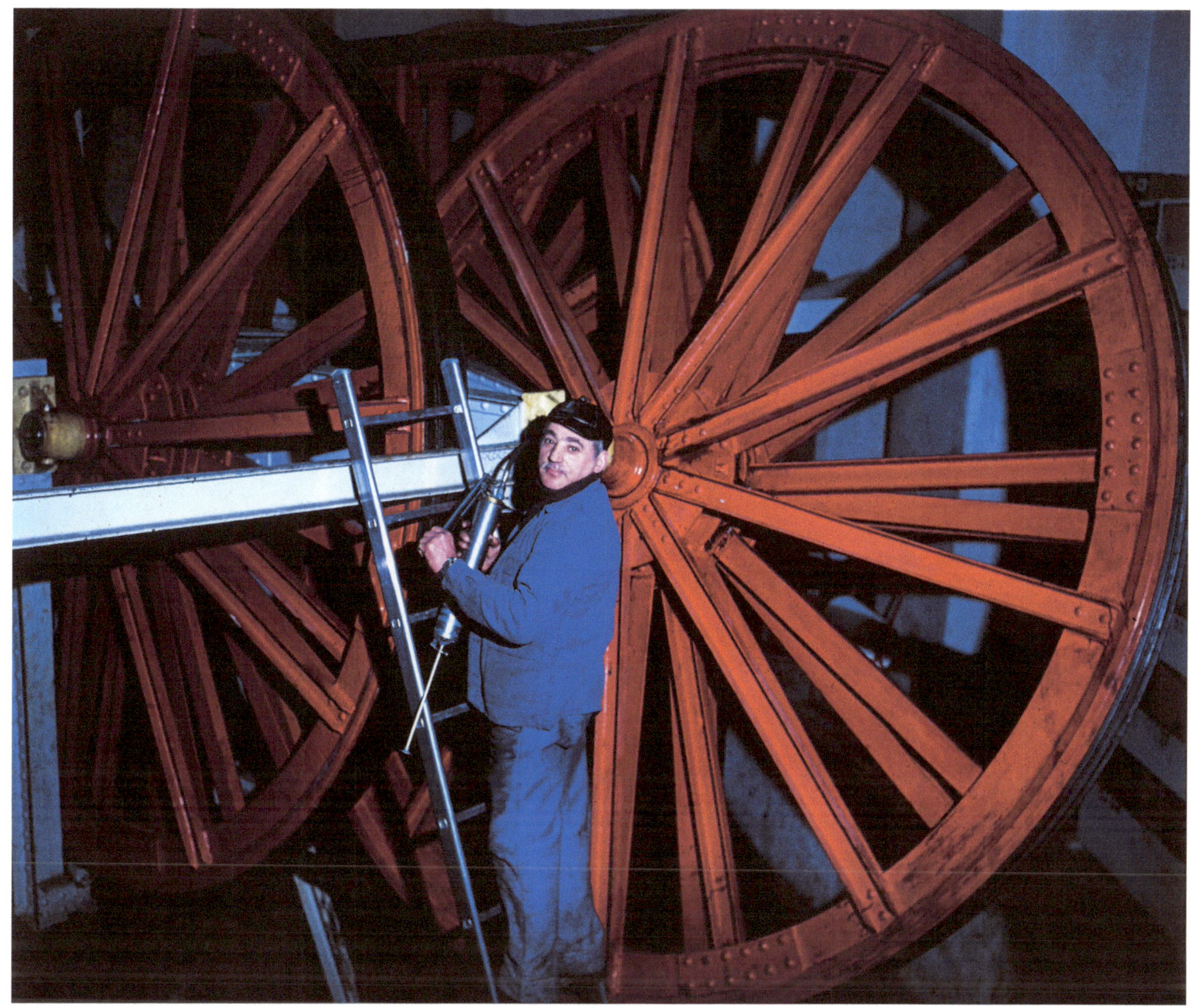

CHAPTER SEVEN: THE EIFFEL TOWER

Like an Iceberg, there is another world hidden under the Eiffel tower that no one gets to see. The motors, pulleys, pumps in engine room that runs the elevators, out of a Jules Verne book are beautiful: an archaic systems that is to be much more efficient than the modern-day electric elevators that share the duty of bringing visitors up from the ground.

Yes, the 100 plus years old hydraulic elevators will take you smoothly to the top. The pistons are actuated by a water circuit with a pressure of 40 to 60 bars, generate motion thanks to three large accumulators of some 200 metric tones each, which provided both the pressurized water reserve, the energy to drive the motion, and the counterweight function.

Each lift is done manually. The operator, Marcel Dupond has been on the job for 30 years. Sitting on a reclined chair in front of big copper wheel he is proudly claiming that if you put an egg at the bottom of the elevator shaft, he can stop the carriage with such precision that the egg will remain untouched.

Above: pulley lubrification

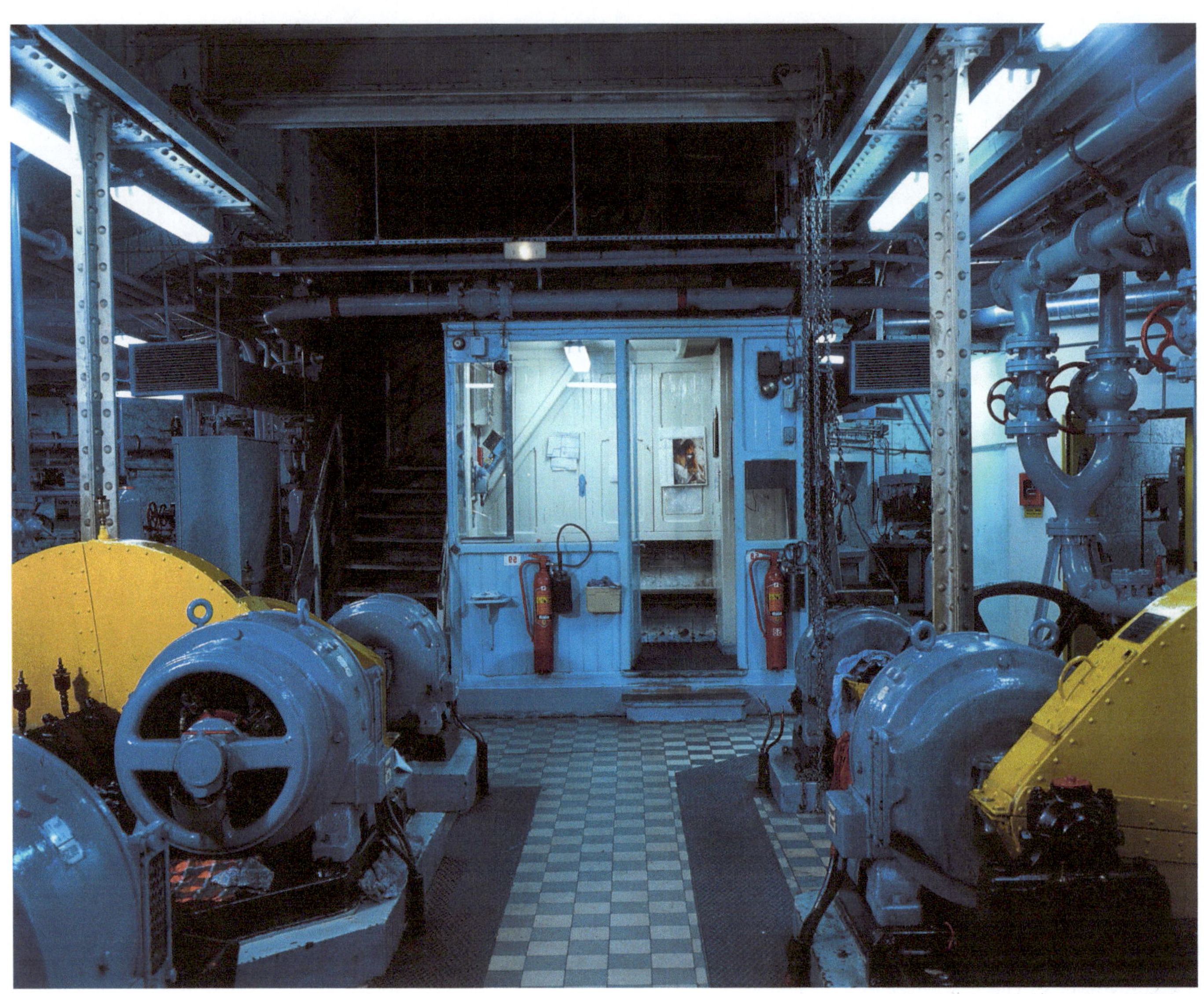

image above: the elevators of the Est and West pillars are hydraulic. Despite their old fashioned appearance they are not of origin. Only the elevator to second floor to the third dates from the creation of the tower. They need to be manually operated.

image right: piston compressing water

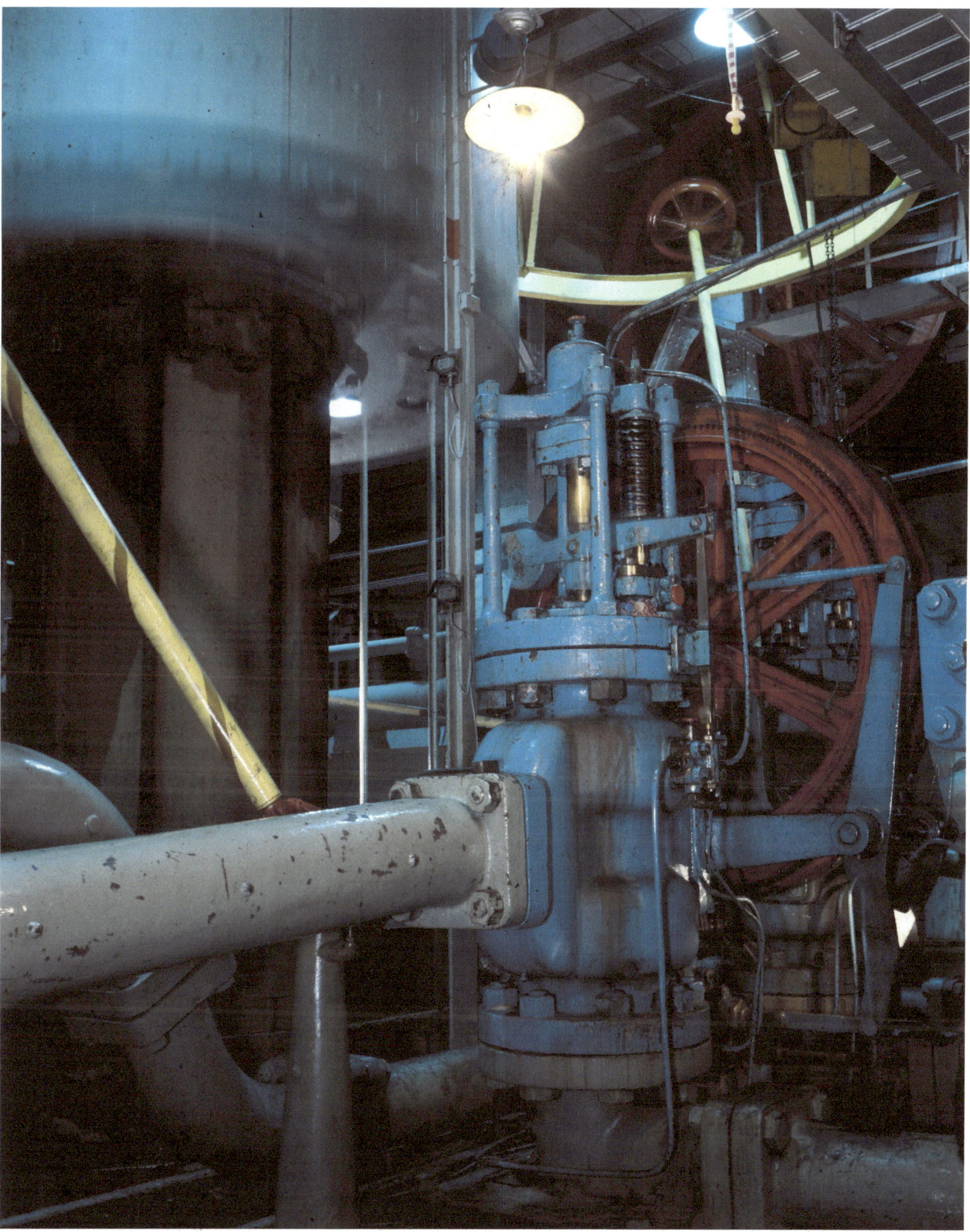

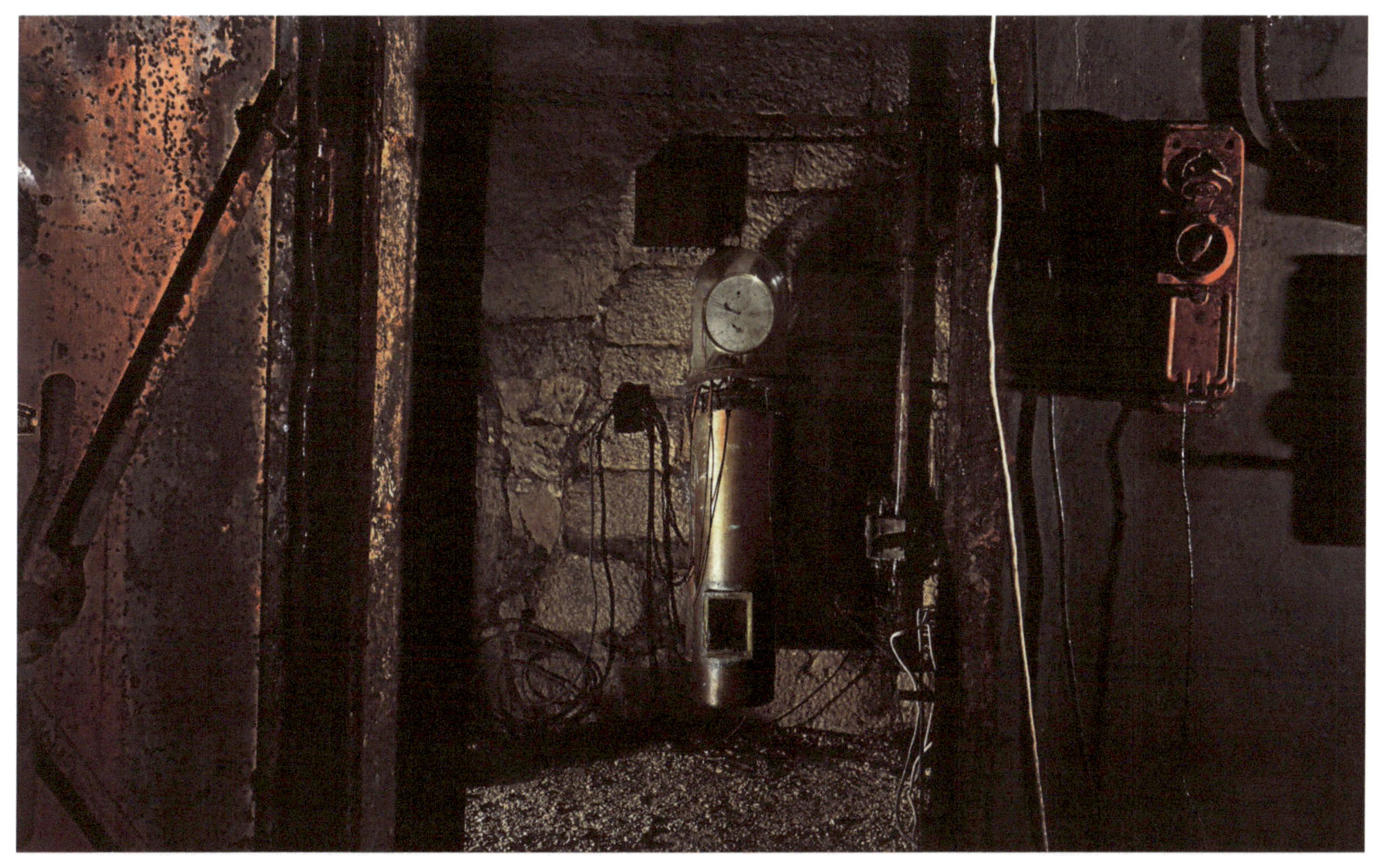

CHAPTER EIGHT: STRANGE PLACES

It is no surprise that the world below the surface of the city, in fact its "negative, has created over the centuries a great number of Urban legends.
Victor Hugo in "Les Miserable's": It was in the sewers of Paris that Jean Valjean found himself.
...Paris has another Paris under herself; a Paris of sewers; which has its streets, its crossings, its squares, its blind alleys, its arteries, and its circulation, which is slime, minus the human form.
The masses regarded these beds of decomposition, these monstrous cradles of death, with a fear that was almost religious, pretty much like a gateway to Hell.
Satanist stories, devilish ceremonies have always been associated with the quarries and the Catacombs. Some are certainly true.
Back in 1775, when it was decided to empty the cemeteries and put the remains of 6 millions corpses in the quarries, the job was done at night, not to anger the population. In reality, for the Church and the law it was a violation of burial grounds.
One can imagine the procession of horses and coaches loaded with bodies and bones silently passing through the dark streets …
Other events have happened under Paris, not morbid but always odd and bizarre.
Here are a few.

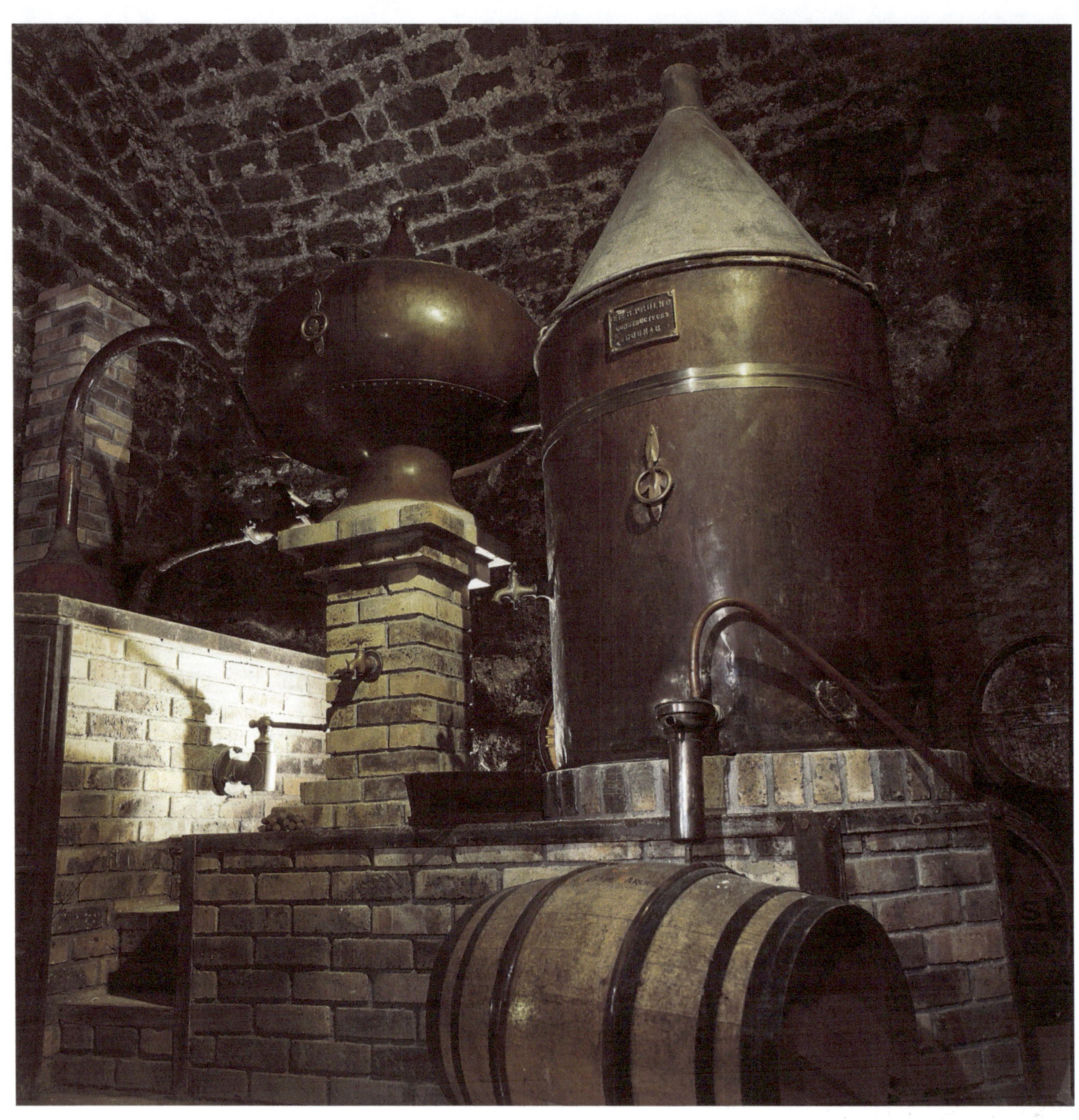

The quarry has been transformed into a wine museum

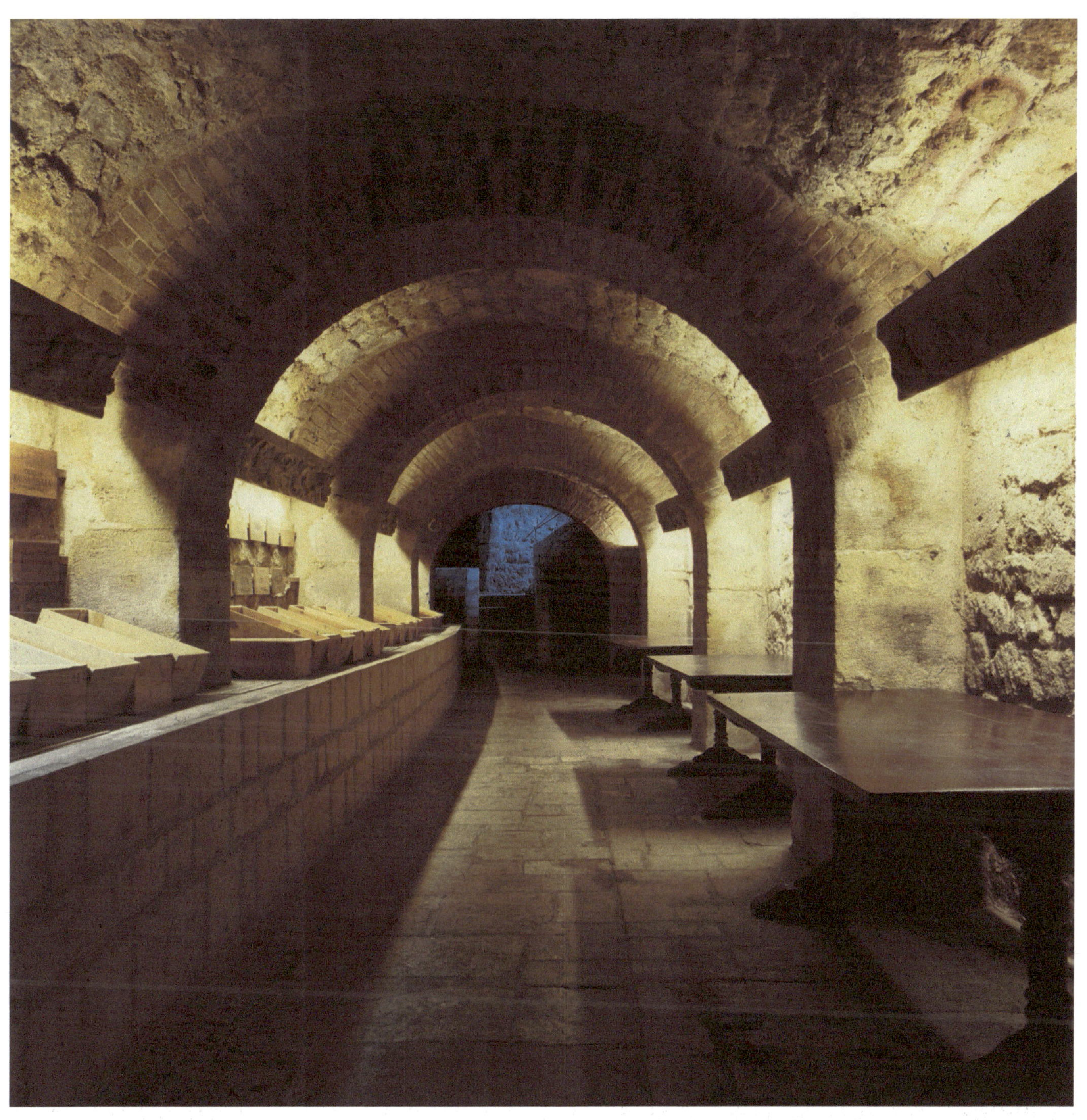

Eiffel Tower's wine cellar situated in the old Passy's quarries

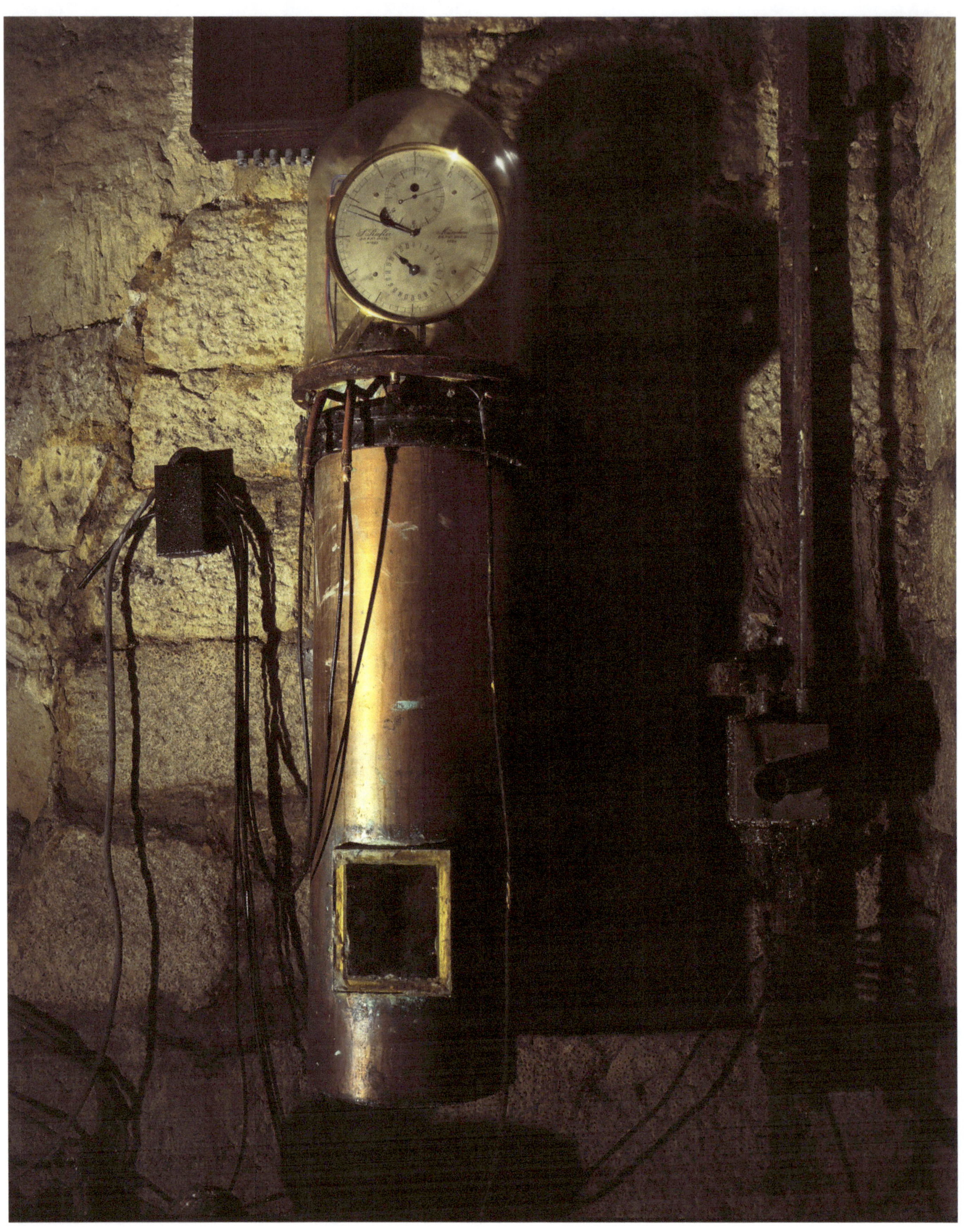

The Time Keeper: original 19th century calibrating clock was located underground.

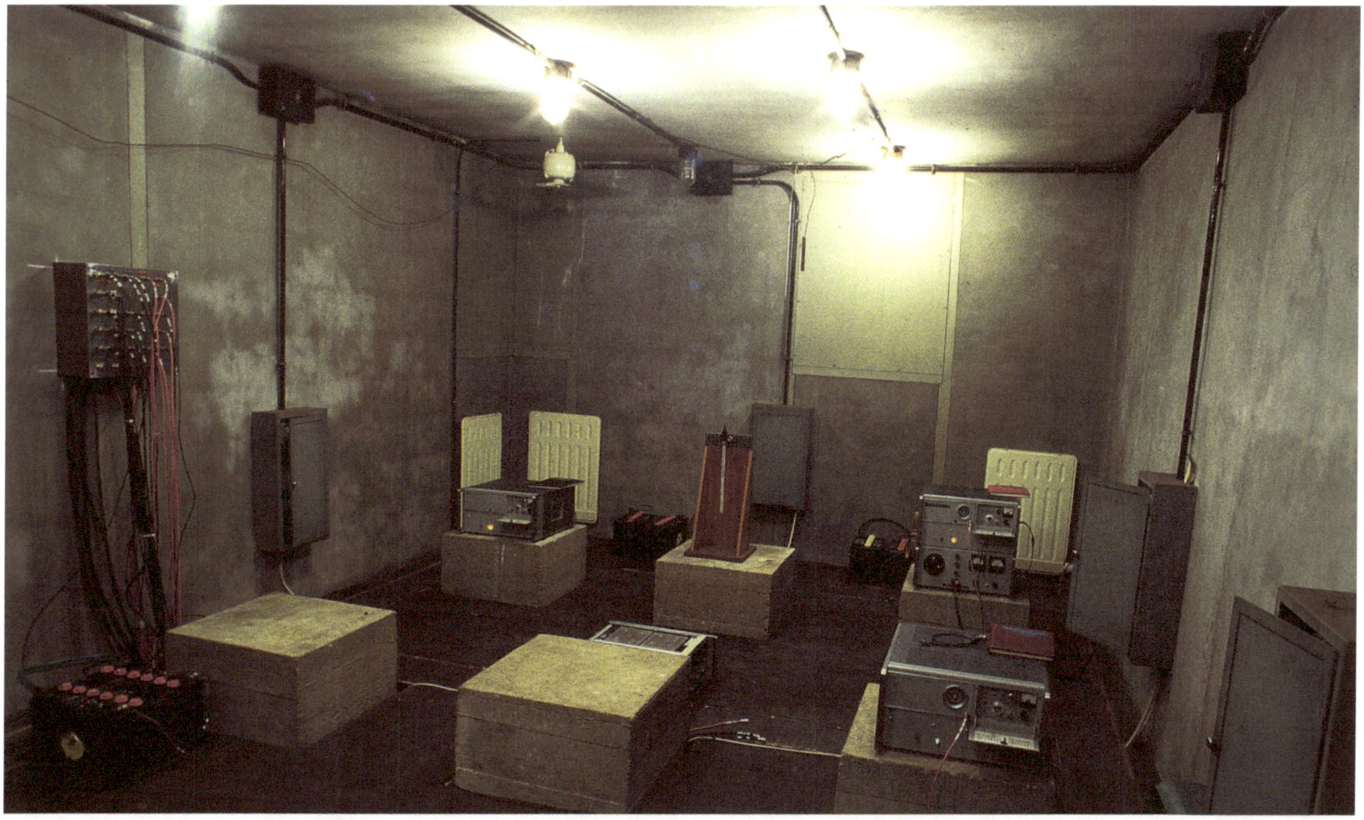

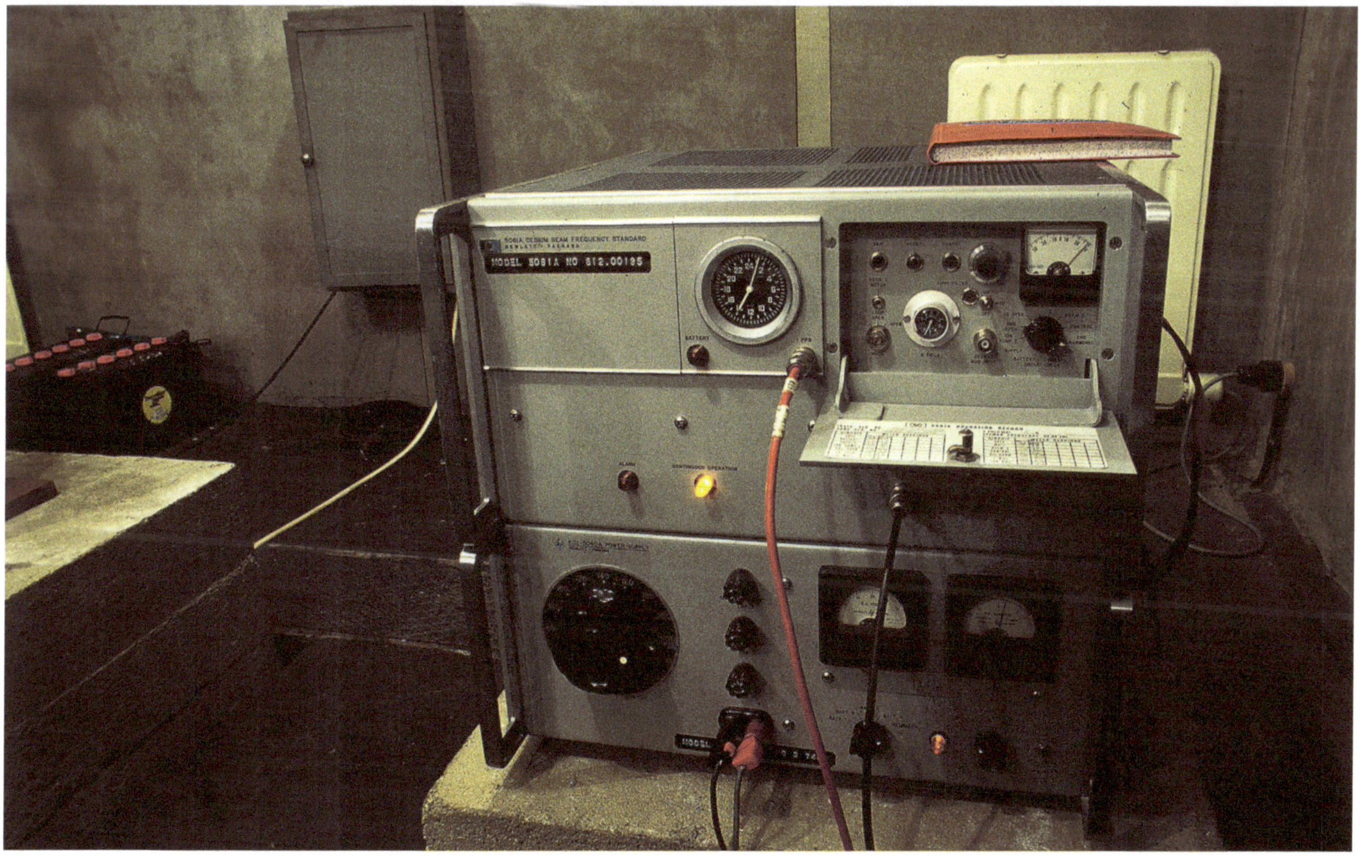

The new Atomic clocks, are located underground.

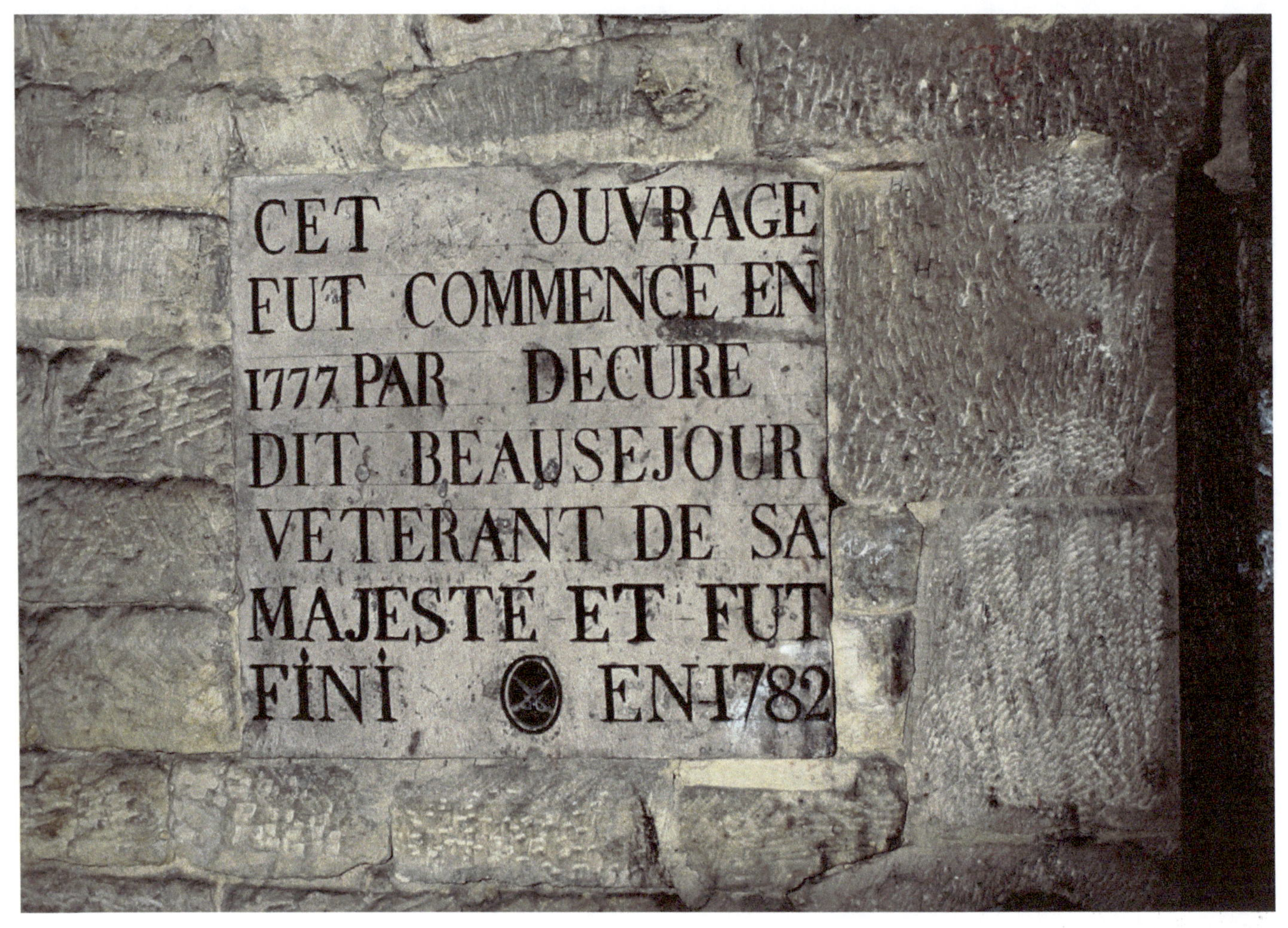

"This work was carried out in 1777 by a man named Decure Beausejour, veteran of Her Majesty, and completed in 1782."

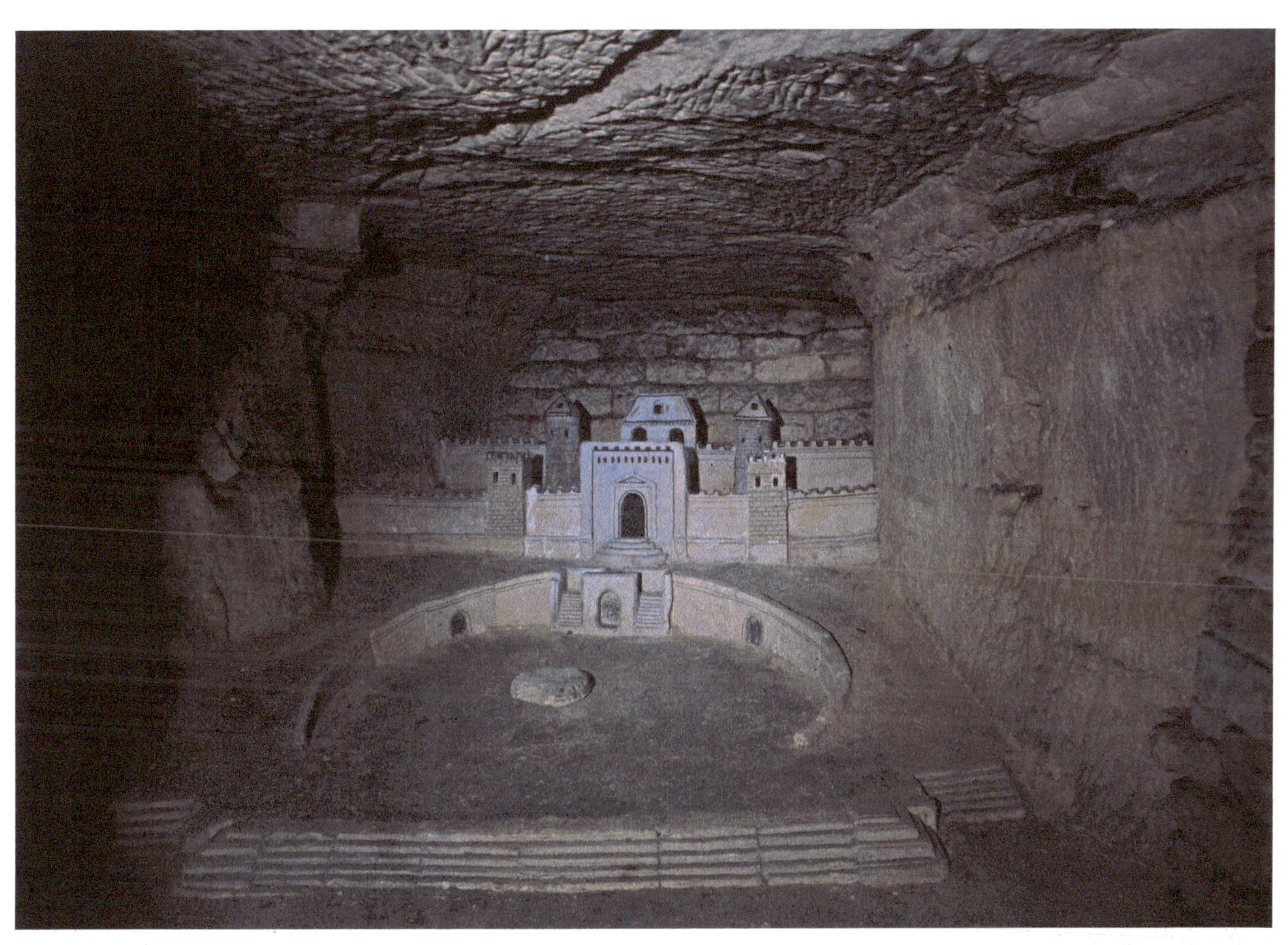

Decure was a soldier of her Majesty Louis XV. He sculpted The Mac Mahon fortress he was watching from his jail in Minocqua in the Balearic Islands where he would have been a time captive by English army. After spending several years working on his masterpiece, he was killed by stones collapsing on him while building an access staircase.

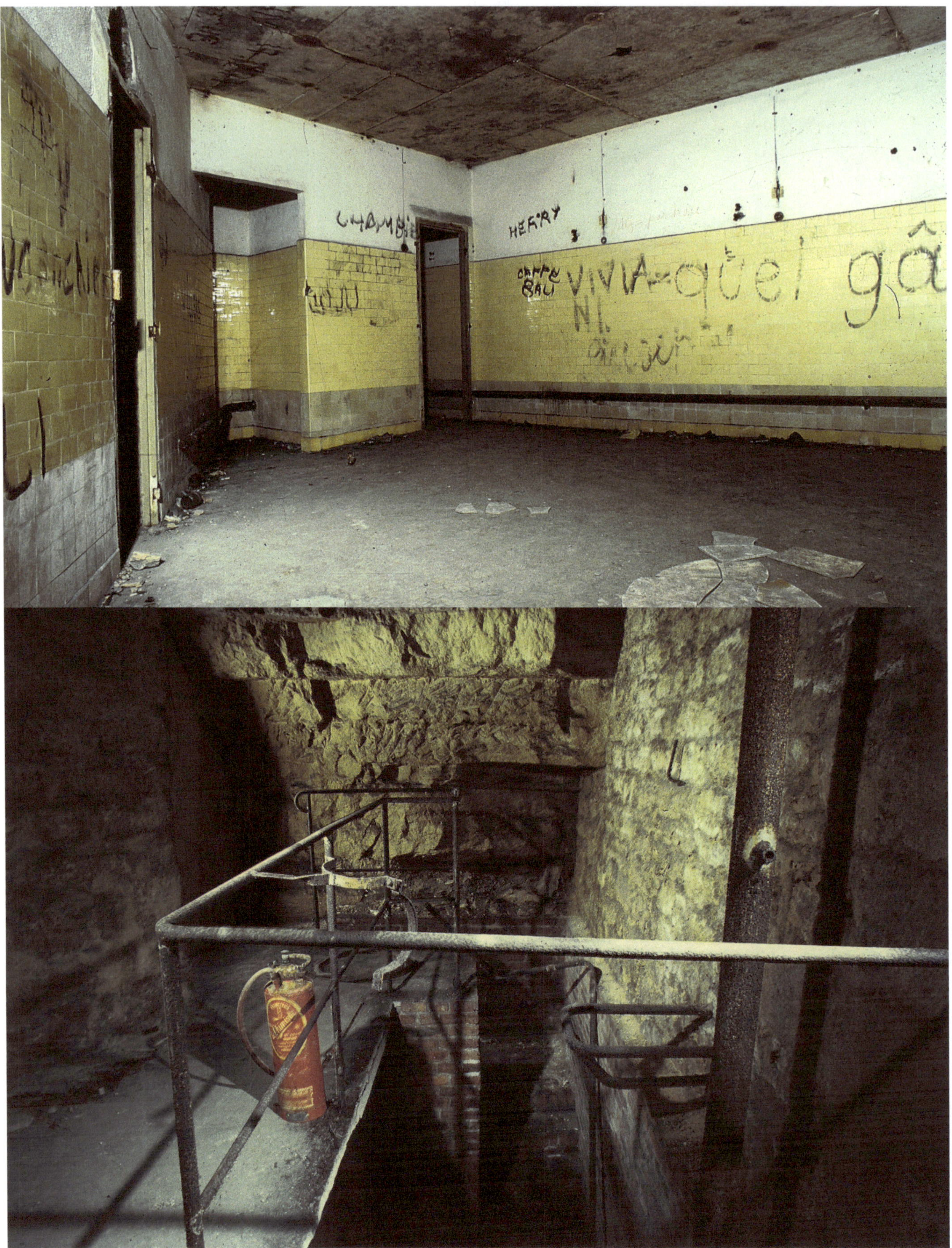
HERRY
VIVIA-quel gâ

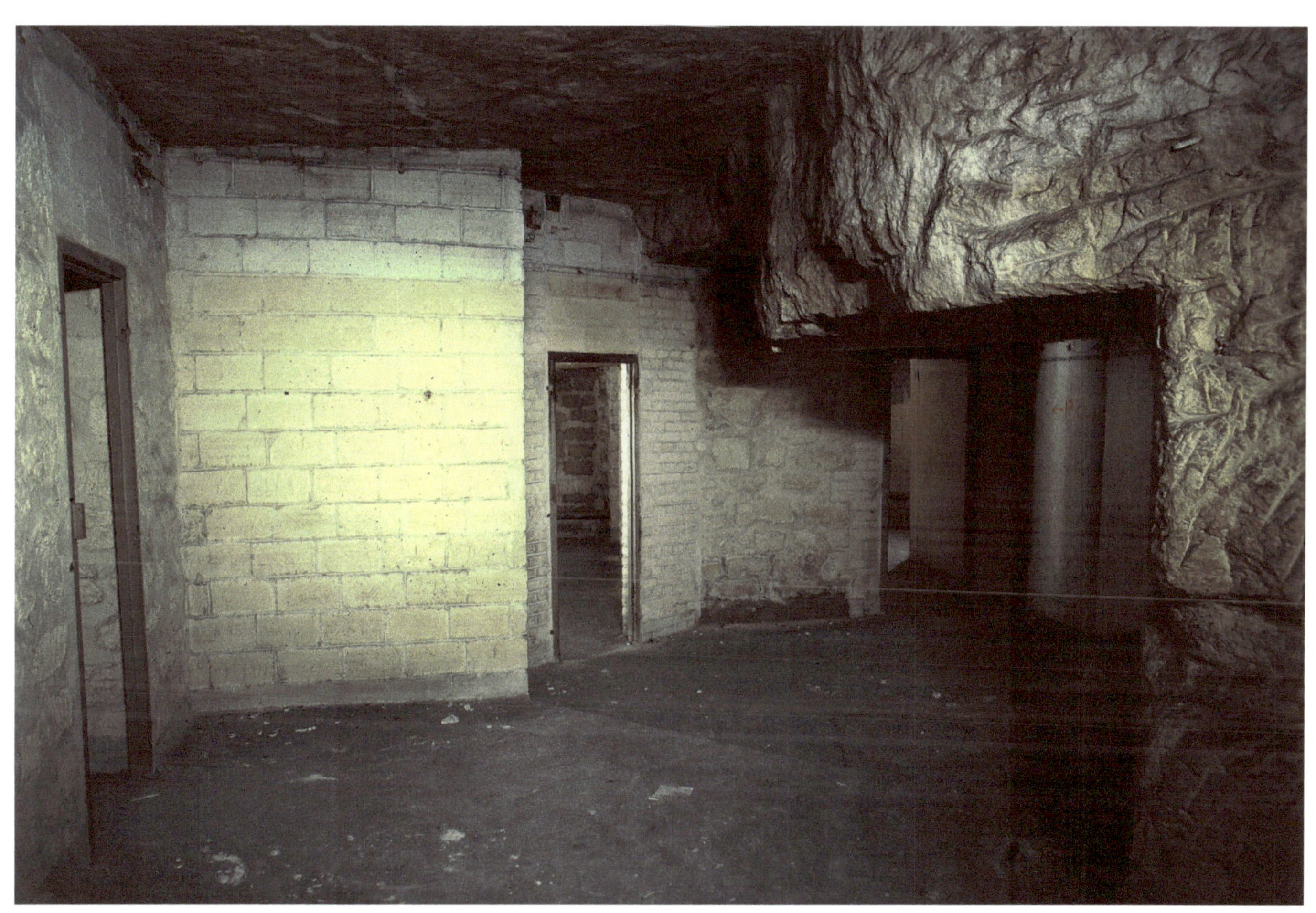

image top: Saint-Anne Hospital's quarries were used to lock up psychiatric patients suffering of "dangerous dementia". The place was called " Cage a fou" (Cage for Crazy).

images left: during the German occupation, the FFI (French freedom fighters) installed a secret headquarters under the Denfert Rochereau place in the 14th district, just under the German Kommandantur

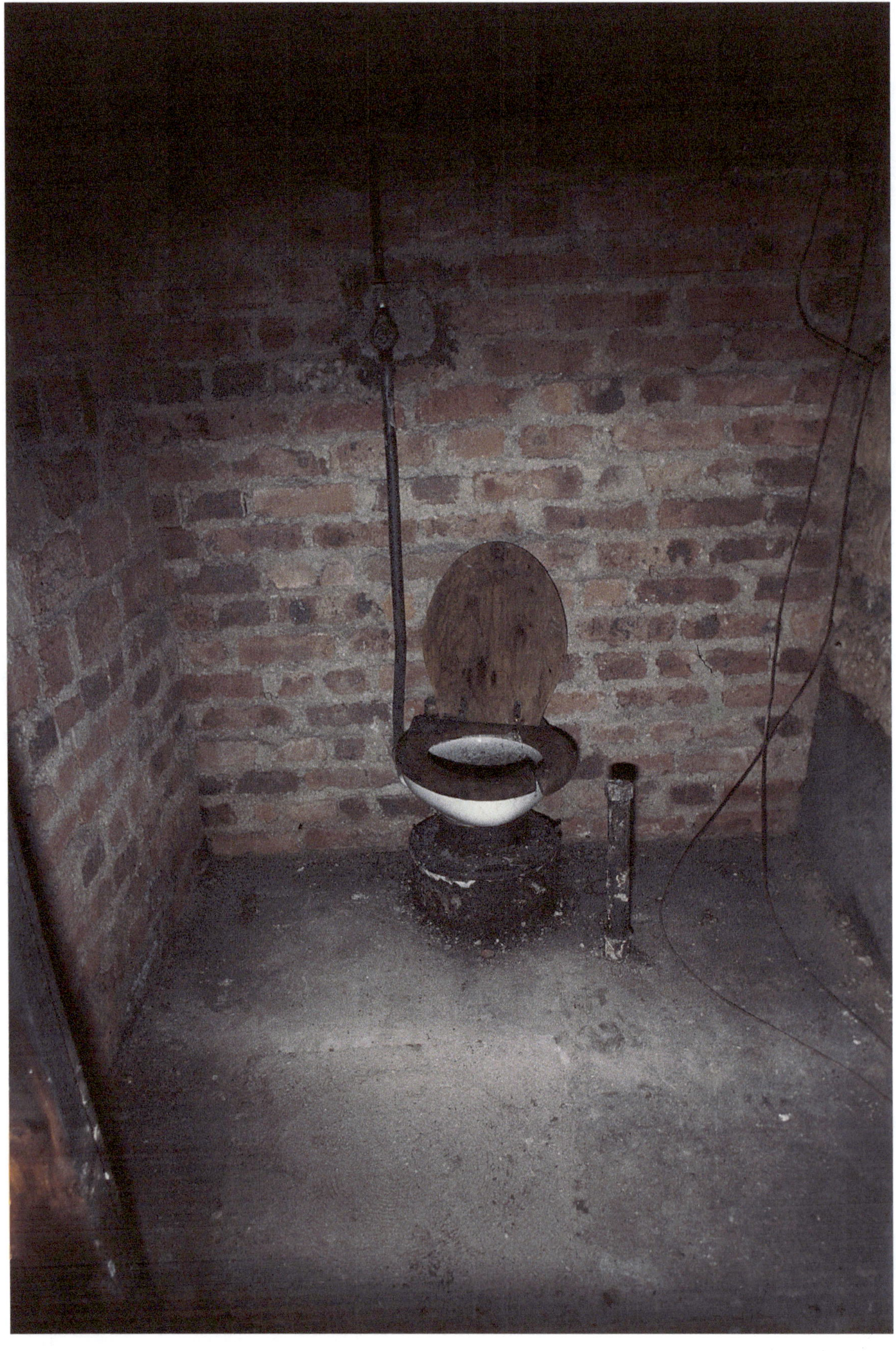

The End

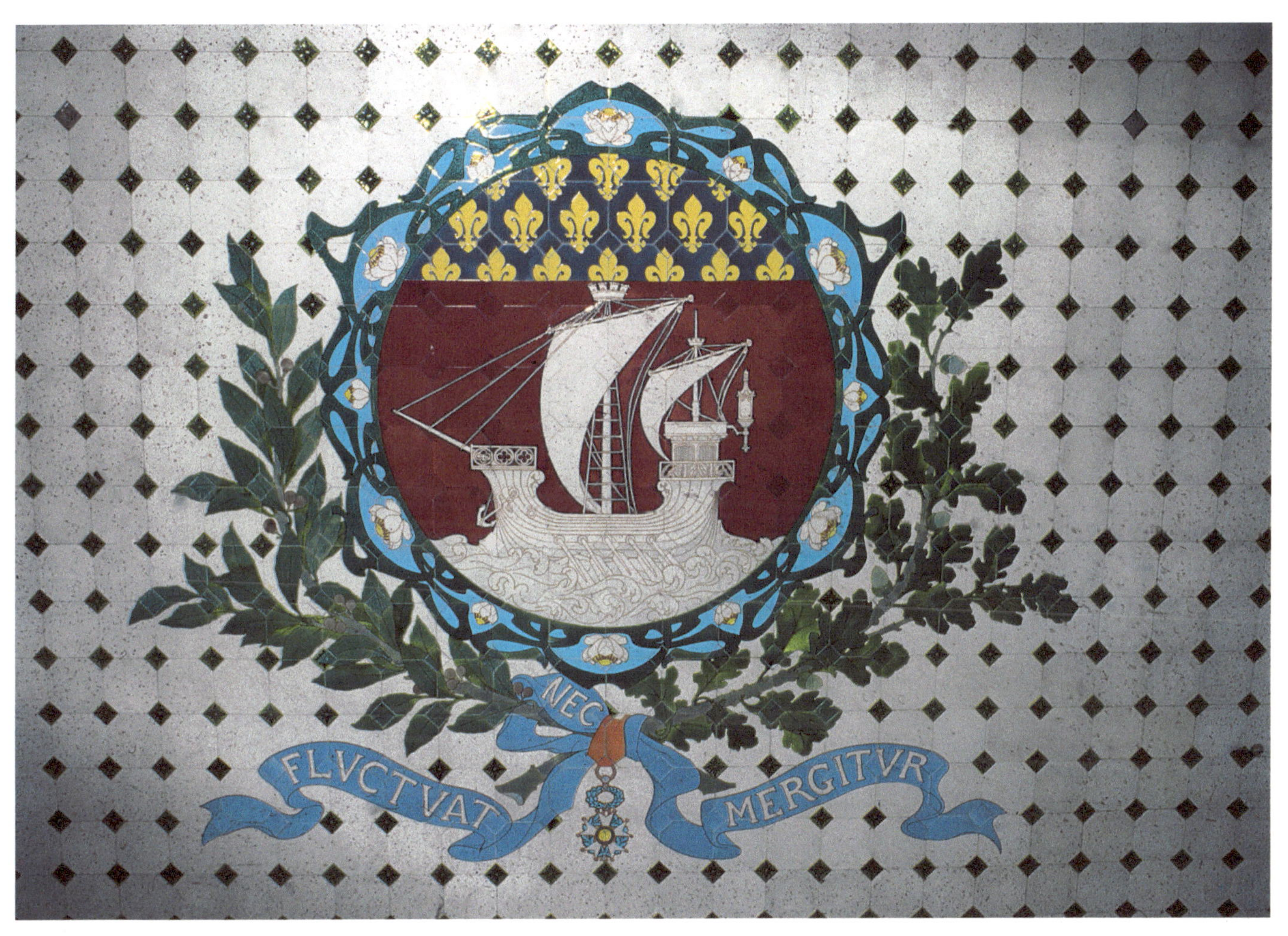

Since 1853, “Fluctuat Nec Mergitur” (Latin phrase meaning “It floats and doesn’t sink”) has been Paris motto. This ancient faience decorates the ceiling of the room where the spring water arrive in the Montsouris Reservoir

Photography and Design by Alain bali
Published by: LA-VIBE PUBLISHING / Hollywood California USA
Tel: 818 636 1859 / alain@alainbali.com
Publisher: Alain Bali - Senior Editor/Production Manager: Jeremy Bali

www.ingramcontent.com/pod-product-compliance
Lightning Source LLC
LaVergne TN
LVHW070134110826
845147LV00002B/253